"In my opinion, Adi Kanda is one of the most talented and prolific artists I have ever met. She is a rare and unique creative force and has become the channel for some of the most beautiful writings to be seen. All of these works seem infused with Love and Truth, and I am always struck by the power, accuracy, and pertinence of these works. These transmissions are tremendous healing tools that can help you on your journey to self-discovery." ~ J.B.

"Adi Kanda's transmissions are very pure, focused communications from a higher plane. I have a Master of Science, had my spiritual awakening 20 years ago, and have been on the inner path ever since. I pieced things together fairly well in that time, or so I'd thought, but now that pales next to what has occurred over a short time due to Adi." ~ M.G.

"To say these transmissions nudged my spiritual path forward by leaps and bounds would be an understatement. Having received many transmissions over the years, I have to say that I've always been incredibly touched by the breadth of personal insight embedded in each. Beyond the words themselves, there appears to be a gentle jolt of healing with each one, coded incomprehensibly for deeper healing, each and every time. Subtle and powerful, they are my favoured tool for consciousness-raising." ~ L.S.

"I can't tell you how often these beautiful words have brought me and everyone who has read them to tears. Just unbelievable." ~ A.S.

"Amazing! I can hear music and voices singing in a church choral setting when I read it." ~ C.F.

"How do you keep producing such beautiful words?" ~ M.H.H.

"It speaks to my heart so clearly, absolutely the truth of what has been going on inside of me. The vibration reaches so deep in me, I have so many tears, not sadness really, a relief that there are now words to describe what is for me. I thank you again so much!" ~ M.L.

"Wow! I'm absolutely blown away by the power of this. It so resonates with my life experience that it's uncanny, and it stirred such strong emotions. I cried a lot when reading it, and then the end felt so empowering and liberating. Adi, thank you, thank you, thank you! It's just the loving message that I need right now. I'm so grateful for your oracular gifts." ~ M.C.D

DEAR
HUMAN
CHILD

DEAR
HUMAN
CHILD

LOVE LETTERS
FROM THE DIVINE
BOOK ONE

adi kanda

AWAKEN VILLAGE PRESS

Editing by: Awaken Village Press
Cover and interior design by: Andrea Gibb

To contact the author or for permission requests, visit:
www.worldwithoutfear.org

ISBN 978-1-957408-20-0 (hardcover)
ISBN 978-1-957408-16-3 (paperback)
ISBN 978-1-957408-17-0 (ebook)

Library of Congress Control Number: 2025908827

Published by Awaken Village Press,
Sioux Falls, South Dakota, U.S.A.
www.awakenvillagepress.com

For Ildiko

"But I, though I saw and heard these things, refused to write for a long time through doubt and bad opinion and the diversity of human words, not with stubbornness but in the exercise of humility, until, laid low by the scourge of God, I fell upon a bed of sickness; then, compelled at last by many illnesses... I set my hand to the writing. While I was doing it, I sensed, as I mentioned before, the deep profundity of scriptural exposition; and, raising myself from illness by the strength I received, I brought this work to a close — though just barely — in ten years... And I spoke and wrote these things not by the invention of my heart or that of any other person, but as by the secret mysteries of God I heard and received them in the heavenly places. And again I heard a voice from Heaven saying to me, 'Cry out, therefore, and write thus!'"

~ Hildegard von Bingen

Contents

Preface

In one of my earliest memories, I am three years of age, sitting on the lap of my sweet, Cornish grandmother at her painted white kitchen table, upon which stood her Underwood typewriter. Lily loved Byron, Keats, and Tennyson and now, together, we were going to write a poem.

The keys were cool metal hollows under my tiny fingers, much too stiff for me to strike, so Granny helped, calling out the names of each letter for every word I spoke. Soon, there it was: the magical apparition of my own poem coming alive before me.

I was writing poetry, and an entire world tumbled onto the paper before my eyes. I saw that this was how people speak with ink. This was the distilled music of words.

For all of my life that music grew in me, through short poems to short stories, to plays and novels, screenplays and essays; and then one night something came through my pen which was absolutely new. It was a voice like no other, and it was not my own.

In January 2000, in the midst of a cold Canadian night, I was asleep with my journal next to my pillow. Now a grown woman and weary mother of three, I was reading Jung and kept the journal close to capture my dreams. I had a sense of the sound of geese calling from who knows where, as if in a winter fog. The morning light came, and there, in my own hand-writing, were words scrawled on top of one another in the dark. Pages of writing of which I had no memory, in a voice unfamiliar to me. Beautiful short lines, foreign and strange.

I have been a writer since the age of three. I knew these words came from another source.

There is a place, a numinous place in between worlds. We touch it when we dream, we touch it when we drink the holy tea or fall deep into a meditation of trust. We know it sometimes when we make love and the experience of union transports us beyond the body, into pure ecstasy. In my sleep travels, I had entered this place, like Lucy climbing into a wardrobe or Dorothy falling into a land of talking scarecrows, lions, and tin men; each one of us on a profound journey toward home.

I had discovered what it meant to drop in between worlds, and my pen recorded the conversation, a communication with a source of higher wisdom, far beyond my own.

Under the soil
the Earth is calling
calling to the seeds who sleep
Asters, poppies
each will grow in time
can you not feel them
Each will one day be Queen
and the beauty is
they know it not
and no one
is Lord
over the other...

These were the first words scribbled in my journal that night, the first stanza of the first oracular poem; writings I would eventually refer to as transmissions, Love Letters from the Divine.

I called this first poem "The Gathering," for it references the great shift which was to come, the days of change, spoken of by so many indigenous prophets and seers of our time.

Children play
do not waken
for dreams are truth
divine
The ancient lives
in the broken seed

In your childhood
know that
you are no better than
the seed
fallen in liberty
as the wild goose calls
hoarse with joy...

Those geese had flown through my winter sleep, calling to me, and emerging through my pen...

We were taught
to question
yet
Ask your mother only one thing

How do I love myself
when I know my
words alone have failed?

I felt such a knowing, such love, in these words.

The words fell like petals as I spoke them aloud, making no sense and yet somehow generating a deep warmth in my heart. I saw the frozen blossom, ice crusted and perfect in its beautiful death. I felt the sticks with their shrivelled leaves and the impulse to gather them up like children in my arms.

What was this forgiveness I was told that I sought, denied by entire worlds? And what was this promise of life, gestating within the earth, waiting to be born? What madness does the child within me whisper?

Decades later, I look back upon this transmission and I see that it speaks to every central principle which would be presented in the thousands of transmissions to come. It was my introduction to the great truths which would arrive to guide me. I would indeed be asked to confront my own anger at any god who could allow great suffering, and I would come to see the vast numbers of souls who walk every day in the confusion of their mistrust.

It was time for awareness to be born; and while most of the words that emerged through my pen would seem to be in English, I came to understand that these writings spoke with a kind of language of their own. Their frequency would penetrate so much more deeply than the mechanics of the words. Their power existed beyond ink on paper. A presence had come to whisper in my ears as I slept, using me as a conduit between the etheric and the waking world.

These writings were not just for me. I was their custodian, their student, their translator; but they were a language meant for the heart of us all.

The morning after "The Gathering" appeared in my journal I called a dear friend, the one person who might not think me mad. Fearless in her spiritual inquiry, Ildiko was immediately enthralled. While I was overwhelmed and confused, she announced that a test was in order to determine the source of the words.

Ildiko and I were part of a small circle of friends who explored a body of metaphysical work known as Master Alignment, which came out of the US in the late-'90s. These teachings were profoundly life-changing for me and for every one of us who received readings in this modality. It was two years after my first reading that my own intuitive awakening took place and beautiful words began to spill out of my pen in the night. I have since spent many years working as a practitioner of the Kore Process, a marriage between the Master Alignment work and the guidance of my own received transmissions.

Ildi proposed that she would ask a personal question about a topic unfamiliar to me, and I would hold the question in my consciousness as I went to sleep. I recall feeling slighted that she had kept secrets from me, but thankfully she had indeed and so a degree of objectivity was possible. The next morning, I awakened to find more pages of words. I stood in my bedroom by the light of the window and read them to her on the phone.

At first there was silence, and then came the sound of sobbing. I asked what was wrong and she said, *"You could not have written these things you have just read to me. I have never told you about this, and there is no way you could have known. So to hear this answer now, I realize I have been heard, and without a doubt, I am not alone. We are not alone."*

If there is one message these transmissions, and all sacred writings, offer to the reader, it is this awareness. We are undeniably, eternally, seen, held, and loved. It is my hope that the Love Letters from the Divine found in *Dear Human Child* will offer this gift to every reader.

In the days following Ildi's revelation, I moved through many stages of my own resistance and fear. Initially I felt violated, as if some unseen force were using me without my consent. Then I too discovered the trust she had expressed, and surrendered to the experience. Almost overnight the meaning, the fragrance, the frequency within the words began to make sense to me. Now I could even read the words I had written overtop of other words in the dark. I knew that my writing, and my world, would never be the same.

I use the term "guides" to name the source of the messages given to me, as it is very clear they come from a realm beyond my conscious knowing. For years I received personal transmissions, and each one would speak directly to the need, to the pain of an individual in their most private thoughts and fears. What this says to me is that we are never without the care and guidance of a higher power, however we choose to name them. It also reminds me of the purposeful nature of our experiences and invites an understanding of the heart, beyond that which the mind alone may conjure.

Please be aware that what you hold in your hand, or are listening to by audio recording, is not just a book. These words are a tool of transformation, meant to be expressed as frequency and used in your daily life as you would practices of meditation, reflection, or prayer. Listen on repeat, read aloud first thing in the morning or last thing at night. Write out stanzas in your own journal or make notes in your book; it is yours to explore. While the frequency is sacred, these words are not precious. They are meant to be used, chewed and digested; chanted, sung, repeated, and memorized. If emotions arise, this is the blessing of release. If intention is stirred, this is the blessing of clarity. Please trust all shades and aspects of the wisdom these words may awaken in you. "Ask, and it will be given to you; seek, and you will find; knock, and it will be opened to you." (Matthew 7:7).

Why Poetry?

One of the first observations I made of those early transmissions was that the lines were very short, and the punctuation minimal. Words where capitalization was expected were often lower case, and out of nowhere capitalization would appear on certain words. Rarely were rhyme or metre noticeable, and yet there seemed to be a flow dictated by the truncated lines which guided the reader.

I found if one thought too much, one could become tangled in the columns, but if one surrendered to the seeming dictation of what was holy, the words flowed and made more and more sense, especially with spoken repetition.

In *Poetry as Spiritual Practice*, Robert McDowell writes: "by meditating and reciting poems, chants, hymns, prayers, mantras, songs and scripture, you make of yourself a tuning fork ready for the thwack of the Divine.

"The Trappist monk André Louf describes this process as a kind of fermentation, a ripening and welling up of the Word 'that has become wholly our own... inscribed deep in our body and psyche. It bubbles up, it flows, it runs like living water.' No matter what you practise, the goal is Reunion with the Word and the shedding of ego, until 'it is no longer we who pray, but the prayer prays itself in us.

Why Poetry?

"Poetry is this reverberating note, this pure sound and shape of your spirit as it makes sense to you at last. Through the almost musical vibration, you move from individual soul out into the Oversoul."

What makes the written word poetic, and how does poetry so profoundly hold communications of spiritual wisdom and healing?

Throughout history, many great spiritual texts have been written fully or partly as poetry: the Psalms and the Song of Solomon of the Old Testament; the Quran; the Bhagavad Gita; the Guru Granth Sahib, the central religious scripture of Sikhism; the Tao Te Ching, the foundational text of Taoism; the Poetic Eddas, Norse pagan sagas; the Dhammapada, a collection of sayings of the Buddha; the Rigveda, one of the oldest sacred texts of Hinduism.

Of course, we know the works of poets such as Rumi, Hafiz, and Emily Dickinson to be rich with spiritual inquiry and expression. The Dalai Lama, Thich Nhat Hanh and Adyashanti have also explored the power of poetry as spiritual expression.

My own humble awakening in some ways parallels the journey of visionary and mystic Hildegard von Bingen. Like Hildegard, I have received words, music, chants, and prayers. She too suffered with physical healing crises and struggled with doubt in the early years of her experience of Divine communication. Both of us were called to reject more traditional paths in surrender to an experience few others understood.

Decades and thousands of transmissions later, the selections in this initial collection have been chosen for their relevance to our extraordinary times, as well as to introduce the range of transmissions which have appeared over the years. Each oracular poem lives within its own context, while together they sing in a chorus of tolerance and trust, addressing some of the most troubling and controversial themes of our day. Most of the transmissions in this volume are dated, but some of the older ones are no longer traceable to an exact date of origin. I trust that they are meant to be timeless.

Dear Reader, as you explore these love letters from the Divine, understand that the words carry a visceral energetic effect, similar to other sacred texts. Throughout my decades-long career in the healing arts, these transmissions have been used in workshops, wellness days, salons, live performances, and as a foundational component of my public programs. They have opened hearts, expanded perception, and awakened long-dormant emotional release.

In the early days of receiving with pen and paper, I did not own a printer; every day I would type out the night's transmission and email it to Ildiko. She would print out a copy for each of us, and she'd study the teachings within, making notes in the columns. Whenever we met, she would pull several frayed transmissions out of her bag to discuss and share.

After her death we found boxes and boxes of transmissions in her bedroom, many annotated: the accumulated treasures of our correspondence. She had lived in a library of divine guidance, the pure expressions with which she was so much at home.

The year before Ildi's death, I experienced a healing crisis of ten-days duration that was a turning point in my life. She was at my side every single day. I was in so much pain and so ill that the veil became very thin. I was given much guidance and several direct commands. One was that I was to begin offering a kind of reading that paralleled the readings I had received in the Master Alignment tradition. A very specific prayer was dictated to me, which I was to use to invite the powerful attunement associated with these readings.

Within weeks of my recovery, I began this new phase of my work, *The Kore Process*, bringing through deep initiations to reveal the karmic patterning of the soul. These intense, detailed, past-life readings are recorded so the initiate may return to them over the course of a lifetime. The Kore work took my clients into such a rich process that I built a program around these readings. It has been a profound honour to serve seekers from all around the globe in this way. Now, having entered my elder years, I see the time will come when my world will once again revolve around the flow of ink upon a blank piece of paper. For me, there is no more joyous place to be.

Ildiko, without you, my scribbled words may have been left to dissolve into time, remnants at the bottom of your purse and mine. You were Jerry to my Esther, and I thank you. I know you bear witness to the birth of this collection, and I know your blessings are upon us still.

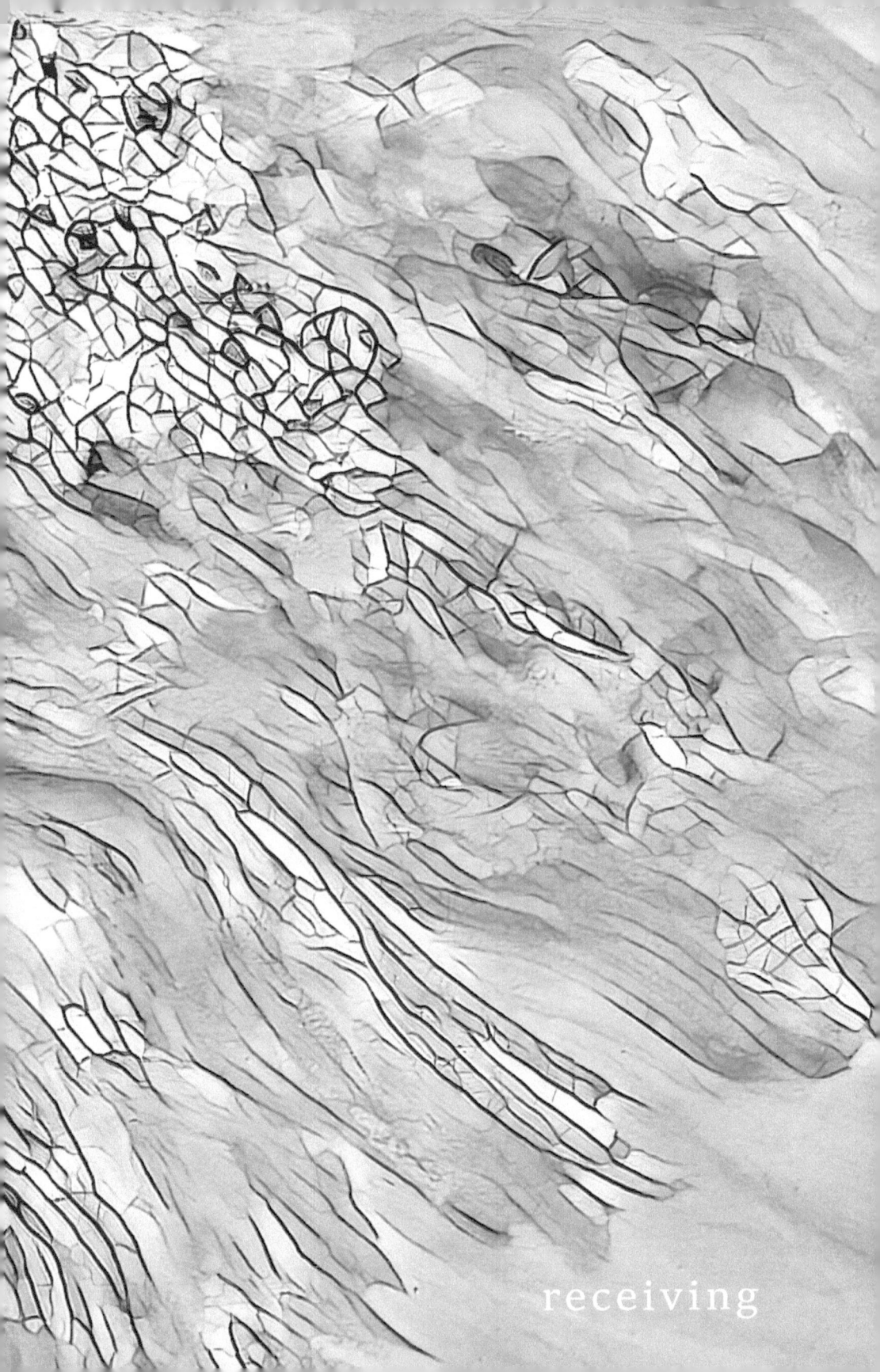

receiving

THE ANNUAL TRANSMISSION
FOR 2019

Are you ready to see
together?

I n recent times, I have received an annual transmission offering guidance for the year ahead; and as this volume is a collection specifically referencing these days of the "Shift," we begin with a series of annual transmissions from the years 2019 to 2024.

This is the only transmission in this volume in prose poem format. Given the unfolding of the Covid years and the subsequent global rise of fear, division, and control, it feels like an important place to begin.

One of the key tenets of the teachings found within the transmission is the understanding that there is nothing outside of Divine order. In the years since this guidance was received, we have all borne witness to the exact chaos described herein.

When we seem surrounded by the dark, it can be challenging to hold our faith in the light. Yet what the transmissions tell us is that the contrasts, the challenges, the shadows of our lives are an exact and perfect catalyst to the evolution we were born to create.

When we prepare to stop fearing disorder, we discover order in meaning. When we trust the path before us, even when it is unclear, we allow ourselves to flow in any situation. It's all in our chosen perception. It is all in how we allow ourselves to see.

If you are feeling overwhelmed by the state of the world, spend time with this transmission. Read it aloud to a friend. Consider it together. There is a powerful magic in the experience of being witnessed, in just the way this transmission tells us that we are not alone and all that is unfolding is within the realm of Creation.

Allow yourself to be seen, and thus, to see.

The Art of Seeing

We are entering an era of personal timelessness. Of absolute inner-forgiveness, of grace. Our sufferings have brought us here.

We are entering a dimensional shift wherein that which once seemed profoundly important becomes meaningless, and that which was once unseen fills our eyes. We will "see" as never before.

In an in-between place, amid changing perceptions of Time, we will learn to forget the half-truths of the material realm and remember to invite the non-physical to return to us.

As we fill with these heightened energies like hot air balloons, some not yet in alignment will combust alchemically and fall away. Souls will shift and depart with growing fluidity, causing confusion and intensity; but we will develop reflexes, trust, and ingenuity. We will discover soul-level potency. We will See together.

Some whose vision is ripened will rise, glorious with unexpected power, and some will come crashing into awakening, a painful but ultimately ecstatic experience. Many will not grasp what is happening at all.

The Art of Seeing

We will be asked to trust even that which seems as dark as a deep winter storm. We will confront what is seemingly impossible and, in this, extraordinary joys will emerge.

Enemies will fight side by side. Beloved friends will part and travel different paths. No assumptions can be made about anything, because nothing is as it was before. We are asked to see.

We will lose patience with information and discover all of it does not need to be analyzed and stored, but that it is much better tasted, digested, and ultimately integrated through creative expression. This is how we will speak what we see.

Emotion will be understood as a language all of its own. Small children will be seen as older than their parents. Elders will begin to return to their potency and leadership. Amongst those who see, ages, genders, and races will become secondary and incidental.

Ideas will be burned alive and go down with their guardians. History will be rewritten or, rather, newly remembered. New understandings will be born collectively, as disparate minds fall into the same awakening, even with different languages and within differing paradigms. We will see with much more than our eyes.

Human reality will begin to become more organically enmeshed with that of the planet, as she lifts herself up before us, daring us to keep looking away. This entwinement will give birth to radical innovation, and that which was once thought miraculous will be brought into being every day.

All developments will be experienced by each individual according to their capacity, which will result in a growing separation of those who see from those who do not, inciting further violent alienation. Yet, it will be within the newly-forged families of commonality, a strong merging of energy fields and loving hearts.

As a species, we will expand into deepened polarization as some elements spin out into nothingness. Aligned elements will then reconfigure again like the loop of an orbit.

The ship is leaving the dock and this incites a rise of unconscious panic; these energies are what the empaths digest when they sleep at night.

There is the same sensation as in a flock of birds flushed from the woods into the sky, seemingly in utter chaos, raising their startled voices and batting their wings. Yet, once aloft, beautiful form and freedom will arise, for they must. This is the way.

The days of being able to actualize what we see through instantaneous creation are upon us. It has always been so, but now we are close enough to witness and draw connections between experience and thought. Like the child who has learned that banging on the piano makes a sound, we are ready now to refine our touch.

We are ready to write the very music which we love the most, to lead our own selves to the dance.

Steps to guide your sight and your freedom:

Practice surrender to both desire and detachment; they are not contradictory, but rather meet one another. Both will lead to wisdom and courage.

Make it your prayer to learn what it feels like to make loving decisions in honour of your own being first, as you are a representative of the Divine.

Every time you begin a new task, resolve to begin from within your own heart, with that open door, that new page, a fresh candle, a patient touch. It matters not what you do in any moment, only the root of Love from which you initiate.

The Art of Seeing

Fear is a vivid call to choice and creation, nothing more. We are exploding into artistry; we are painting and writing our being-ness in this moment, right here now.

Fear taunts us like the fans of an opposing team to ask: do we dare, do we dare, do we dare?

These are the days of dimensional fluidity. We are given a clear choice to either intentionally, consciously stand up in the shoes of the Creator, or be swept away in the hurricane, the eruption, the flood. The choice is ours.

Love is not a lie. It is what allows us to be one of those who see.

THE ANNUAL TRANSMISSION
FOR 2020

The power and purpose of
polarity.

This was a year when humanity turned a corner into a dark age. In our fear of the shadow, we want to hide. But what if darkness is the very catalyst required to awaken us to the light?

In my own processes of cleansing cellular memories of pain, I have witnessed the darkest of moments become beautiful before my eyes. I have watched as yin dissolved into yang and they became one whole, shadow and light as partners in the creation of wholeness.

As a highly sensitive child, I had many experiences of connecting to subtle realms in my dreams and waking moments. Nights were often difficult; I had recurring nightmares and vivid images were often presented to me in the shadows of twilight. There was one particular being who came to visit often, a grey gargoyle who used to hover in the upper corner of my room, leaning against the ceiling as if he were sitting on an invisible perch. He watched me from this place as if he were my keeper, as if he wanted to be seen. He was waiting for something, and all I wanted was for him to go away and never return.

He stopped coming to me by the time I reached adolescence, when other kinds of turmoil entered my dreams. Many years later, in the midst of a process of deep energetic release, he returned one last time. I was soaking in the bath, weeping and confronting familiar emotions of self-blame and doubt, when I looked up and there he was. This night he perched right on the edge of the tub, close enough for me to touch him. He looked deep into my eyes and what I found there was a desire for love. He had been waiting for my love all this time.

That day I began the journey of letting go of the belief that some part of me was shameful, toxic, and dark. I discovered that my gargoyle was the face of the monster I feared lived inside.

A new understanding of the role of the shadow is the invitation of our times. Read this transmission aloud when you feel caught in the negativity of daily news. Allow these words to bring you back into an understanding of Divine order. There is nothing outside of Source. There is nothing beyond the power of Love.

* You will notice the last lines of this transmission refer to death. Read these words with the understanding that death is neither negative nor positive, but rather offered as a polarity in our material realm, so that we may have another chance (and another and another) to revisit our rejected or bypassed opportunities for expansion. This applies to each one of us on a personal level and to our collective experience as a whole. We also must learn to die to our own illusions, in order to be reborn.

Manifesto

The era of reunion
has begun

This is a time of remembering
our highest nature
a remembering of who we are
as never before

This is a time of falling deep
into the mirror of
revealing our own shadow
as the severed Self
is reclaimed

These are the days of movement
as our eyes are opened
to all we have been afraid
to see
the days
of dancing on the head of a pin

DEAR HUMAN CHILD

as any misalignment
will no longer be tolerated
within the individual
within the walk
across nations and continents
upon the crust
of our world

These are the days of choice
of the wizard revealed
behind the curtain
of coming to know separation
as an illusion
we can choose
to end

These are the days of the greatest ignorance
standing next to the revelation
of the truth
the days of the pendulum swing
of having travelled so far from what is real
we cannot help but be pulled
magnet to Source
back toward the union we have lost

These are the days of profound humility
as we fall to our knees
before our own foolishness
and yet answer this same horror
with encompassing love

This is the time of a new and perfect vision
as all we have been afraid to see
comes into focus
before our eyes

Manifesto

the days of
fear made manifest
of the shadow fighting for its life
under the light of a rising sun

These are the days of walking blind
because we are learning to see
with our hearts

These are the days of disasters
and miracles
of becoming lost so
we may return home
of witnessing the wound
so that healing may come
These are the days of total destruction

of what cannot live in separation
for wholeness must rise again

This is a time of remembering our agreement
to walk away from ourselves
so we may recognize the God within
from afar

These are the times to realize
that either we must choose to stand
in our higher nature
or there is nothingness

Either we see the Divine in one another
or we are blind
Either we make Love

or we die

THE ANNUAL TRANSMISSION
FOR 2021

An anthem of Oneness and a
call to reunion.

This transmission takes us deeper into an exploration of duality as a fundamental and purposeful expression of Divine Energy. How perfect that our universe itself is made up of such great darkness and such great light.

While giving birth to my first child, in our small one-bedroom walk-up in the heart of Toronto, I was instantaneously introduced to this principle. Labour began strong and hard for me. There were no hours of wandering around the house undulating like a goddess and sweetly puffing through contractions. Despite all the prenatal classes, I felt completely unprepared for the amount of pain I experienced and was immediately overwhelmed, but just as quickly my guides whispered in my ear:

"You are in fear," they said, "and you want to run. Don't go there, it will make things worse. Turn around, turn around. Move toward your pain, rather than away."

They were right. The fear of being in a body that was facing many hours of such intensity compelled my starborn spirit to want to leave, to dissociate. But in my gut I knew I had to trust, and when the next contraction hit I brought all my concentration inward and visualized diving into the locus of my pain, my own cervix and the surrounding musculature, all working to open and allow the birth of my baby. This act of surrender created an immediate shift in the way I experienced the pain. It was still present, but without the influence of fear: the razor sharp ferocity diffused and I began to work with my body instead of against it. I began to trust the messiness of my humanity and work with my own being instead of against the forces of the natural will. I was at peace with my experience, no longer afraid. It changed everything and my baby was born plump and healthy as the May sunshine streamed into our room.

My body and my psyche seemed to learn from this experience, as my second and third children were born with labours that lasted minutes, rather than hours. I know women who experience truly ecstatic labours, so great is the depth of their surrender. Of course, every labour is unique; but, whatever our journey, I have always felt that we mothers are blessed to live the experience of giving birth as a perfect template for the process of awakening. We enter into the deep unknown in order to know new life. If we dare to give ourselves over, to become one with the experience, we move through our fear and emerge transformed.

Life brings this opportunity to us all, through the teachings of our pain, our shadow, our fear. When we listen to our own higher guidance, even our greatest darkness may be transformed.

Turn around, turn around. Move toward your pain, rather than away.

Singularity:
The Days of One

Astronomers have spoken
of holes that are black
and endless
amidst galaxies
massive in their brilliance
These holes
are nothing more
than the inversion of such a light
They pull us in
because they must
because it is the will
of the Collective Soul

When it is our turn to tumble
to slip and fall
we try so hard to hold on
to the edges of our world

and yet we hang
upon the event horizon
a position of no return
We are crucified in that moment
as in desperation we do
everything we can
to grasp on
to stay where we are
to remain in the familiar
the known
the old

But it is the purpose
of black holes
to consume us
and so we must eventually surrender
as there is nowhere else
we can possibly go

As we plunge
into visible oblivion
there is no more pretend
no more denial
The immediacy of terror
snaps us free
from cables and strings
and wires
from attachment of all kinds
to everything we think
we need

And that moment of confronting
absolute death
absolute fear

Singularity: The Days of One

becomes the lightning strike
to freedom
The hole speaks to us
and says
by relinquishing yourself
to me
you set yourself free

Thus this moment
leads us to understand
the darkness cannot
be bypassed
but rather is
the very means
of our enlightenment
and then we say
yes
I let go
In this moment
the Fall
is my destiny

And there
in that breath
is born the magic
the dreaming open-eyed
If we are watching
an image of the self
spinning into a well
of absolute darkness
then the spin
the spiral becomes
like the tail
of a rotating comet

DEAR HUMAN CHILD

as she lights up
from within
the radiance growing
toward an explosive light
which changes everything
about what lies
at the bottom of eternity

Imagine
as the brilliance penetrates
the dark
the hole itself
is turned inside out
and we have died
for the very purpose
of coming back to life

Can you see
how the heart of tragedy
must lead us
to encompassing love?

Here we are
in the midst of the deadfall
and yet at the same time
tasting the brilliance
even as we are learning
how to release it
from within
Here we are falling
Here we are spinning
into galaxies

Singularity: The Days of One

Here we are

The year of the One
has begun

The year of the One
has begun
The time of two
is done
As we choose to see the world
through the One
we will find ourselves
and the purpose
of these days
This is a place available to us
thus do we sink
into godliness
even as the winds of cleansing
rage all about us
for what is lost
makes way
for the presence
the very essence
of what must be regained

We have not told the truth
to ourselves
for a very, very long time
Now we must
Now it is time

DEAR HUMAN CHILD

We said
our world is material
limited
and must be controlled
to be survived
We said
dominance is the answer
science is the answer
industry is the answer
technology is the answer
if only we silence the heart
if we can become
the machine
we can surpass the death
we fear so greatly
and we can pretend to be
the God we created
in the image
of this fear

We said
we are separate
the good from the bad
the takers
from the ones who have lost
the white from the black
from the yellow
from the red
The men who must own
from vast Mother Earth
who continues to give
We said we were either
the chosen ones
or not

Singularity: The Days of One

We said we were the self
who sought freedom
and the problem was the other
We said
we were two

And so our visible world
has responded to our command
that which we sought
in our emptiness
that which we believed
in our fear
has become our truth
it became the truth
of the lie
of two

In our terror of death
we burned what was alive
In our fear of hunger
we ate what was not food
In our fear of sickness
we created an epidemic
of confusion and disconnection
In our fear of lack
we created hoarding
and financial collapse
In our loneliness
and firm belief in separation
we created isolation
such as never before

In our fear of fear
we have made ourselves blind

to dimensions of being
larger and more real
than the games of this world
and yet
all this
all this is the way
the only way toward the One

We must walk
the path of division
we must taste
the absence
we must witness the death
we must walk
in a vulnerable body
to know the way
to return
to the infinite One
And now
that day is here

This state
this experience of one-ness
is not simply metaphysical
but rather expresses
in every moment
It is an opportunity found
in every corner
of your world

What are the words?
How do we speak
what is now becoming
the One?

Singularity: The Days of One

To the political enemy
I see you
I see me in you
I thank you
I love the you that is in me
In this way
our separation ends

To poverty in the material
I see you
I see me in you
I thank you
I love the you that is in me
In this way
our separation ends

To illness in the body
I see you
I see me in you
I thank you
I love the you that is in me
In this way
our separation ends

To the food on the plate
To the rivers and the oceans
To the crying child
To the terror in the night
I see you
I see me in you
I thank you
I love the you that is in me
In this way
our separation ends

DEAR HUMAN CHILD

This
our undying principle
of all existence
will awaken us
in these times
as we return to witnessing
the One
even as we still walk
in bodies of two and two

As we open our eyes
to this knowing
so much will be revealed
so much we have tried
to understand with our minds
will be spoken to
by the ever-knowing
of the Great Heart
which is One
One Spirit
One Source
One Being at all times

In the days to come
we will begin to understand
how the Earth can heal
like magic
reborn into her state
of Oneness
with all skies, seas and lands
whole
rich
and interwoven once again

Singularity: The Days of One

How the teachings of
great wisdom sites
will speak to us
The pyramids
the crop imprints
the portals between dimensions
these we may now allow
to communicate with us
in the language
of One

How illness of body and mind
is not what we have believed
but rather expressions
of our greatest dualistic fears
and the more we name
the virus
the disease
the pain
as something outside of ourselves
the more it will find us
play with us
in the great revelation
of the One to come
We will open our eyes
to witness
both the vastness of the fear
through which we have created
and then the ease
with which we reclaim
these powerful
raging
disassembling
parts of ourselves

DEAR HUMAN CHILD

We may only know how to claim
the light of the One
as we dare to digest
the size of the shadow
of our All
as we dare to comprehend
the lights of a thousand suns
extinguished
darkness beyond our old imagining
when we can witness
this too
within our own being
then we are ready
for a hundred thousand suns
and more
to be revealed
as the One Sun
that we are

I see you
I see me in you
I thank you
I love the you that is in me

In this surrender
of ownership
of control
of need for acknowledgement
of fear of any lack
I see you are enough

I am enough
we are enough together

The season of the dying

Singularity: The Days of One

melts into the warming soil
seeds of the infinite One
You now stand
invited
to listen to the children
to the elders
to connect
to communicate
beyond the physical
to meditate and pray
before all else
to act only and always
when inspired by connection
to relinquish doubt
and distraction
to care less
and immerse more
to witness the universal beings
the invisible forces of the One
everywhere now
for they can no longer
be denied

For the vortex of
the hole of nothingness
has called us within
until we spin
strands spiralling into union

Beginning now
yesterday and tomorrow
Singularity
The All
has always
been enough

THE ANNUAL TRANSMISSION FOR 2022

Are you ready to create?

For water to transform into steam, it must first reach a boiling point, a churning, foaming, heated rebellion wherein it refuses to remain liquid and by leaving its old form behind, rises into the expansion of mist and fog. This is, in a way, the experience of our times. We are reaching a tipping point, a culmination of critical mass, rich with the opportunity of transformation. It is not so much that we are asked to fix the old, but rather that we are offered the chance to step through dimensional awareness and leave our previous world behind.

In some ways, this alchemy is an understanding beyond words, one simply to be lived as illusions fall away. The mirage dissipates, and we are astonished at what we once thought was real. Our naked emperors parade before us; and beyond the shock we begin to recognize the scent of liberation from our own ignorance. Instead of falling into fear of loss, we learn to trust what we may not yet understand and simply let go. Instead of panicking about the state of the world, we begin to observe patterns of the shadow rising to be released. Instead of feeling hopeless that things will never change, we begin to understand that the power of the Shift lies within each one of us. Perception becomes intention. That which we are ready to allow may begin.

When you read a transmission aloud, note that the line endings create punctuation and rhythm. I believe they are received in this format to encourage us to find our own flow as we speak them and bring the frequency within the words into form.

To the See

When the wave rises
we cannot say
the exact moment
it will crest
and begin its fall to freedom
into wholeness with the infinite

So ask not
are we done?
ask not
are we here yet?
but rather soften into
all flow
and do not judge
your arc
your ride

You witness
such shifting sands
your vision blurs

To the See

in the heat of the sun
you are unsure
if you are dreaming
if the shadows
upon the horizon
are real
or true

Everywhere you turn
you wonder
if this is the godly way
or if this is the illusion
the bed of lies
which makes one a fool

Those whom you once trusted
seem to collapse
as if they had always
been made of dust
and those whom you once judged
surprise you
as they crack open your heart
and reshape your soul

Nothing remains
in the realm of the ordinary
Nothing is as it used to be
for the story is now told
across fields of light
through layers and layers
of dimensions
cutting consciousness
beyond space
beyond measure

DEAR HUMAN CHILD

beyond a world of
day and night

Just when you think you know
you realize you don't know
Just when it starts to make sense
it doesn't anymore
and we begin to recognize
that we are no longer alive
in the realm of
experience which marks us
We are being born instead
into a realm
of truth as constant creation
beyond categorization
beyond constructs of old

Look into the eyes
of your brother
and you may find alive within him
the dark fears
of an abandoned child

Look into the eyes
of your enemy
and you may find a hidden wisdom
a soul who has simply learned
how to survive

Look into
your own eyes
and allow yourself to see
as if for the first time
the clutter of
persona and denial

To the See

For there is no more time
no more use
for addictions of distraction
not another moment to be given
to doubt or blindness
not another day to spend
in helplessness
hopelessness
or fear

For whether this is
your last day upon
a hellish Earth
or your first day
in a Heaven of your own making
it matters not
The wave has arisen
the wave has arisen
and it will return us all
to the See

The time has come
to cease thinking with the brain
and instead infuse
your presence with expansive sight
to stop breathing
with the lungs
and instead inhale
the force of a destructive and creative fire
to walk upon the soil
and at the same time
transcend the doing of it
all the while discovering beauty
in every particle

of your sleep-walking
day-dreaming world

As you expand
slowly, slowly exploding the DNA
as you breathe in
this fiery light
you may believe
that now you have drunk the tea
taken the pill
but this
dear children
this is your return to knowing
the remembering
of the coming
of the end of the night

This is exactly how
the key is handed back to you
placed firmly in your hands
for you can never cease
human confusions
without first naming the stories
the stage and the players
and then bow
in absolute gratitude
as you rise up
as you re-materialize
into your entirety
and leave those stories
behind

This is the melding
of a transporting state

To the See

wherein we envision
ourselves into alchemy
with the material voice
of our human drama
We the wordsmiths
we the players
we the audience
and the critics on opening night
forever and forever at play
caught between suffering and joy
hide and seek
with the light of utter
absolution and forgiveness
allowing ourselves to be found
allowing ourselves to be found
and the game is thus done
the dissolving forces
of negative illumination
collapsing inward
until we cannot be lost
confused
or distracted again
no matter how great the storm
no matter how deep
the crashing of this giant wave

Come here
to this shore
one, two, three times
every day
Let the reminder
of meaning within chaos
sing in your ears
and become

one of the ones who has
relinquished fear
and found the rhythm
of acceptance
the untouchables
the transformers
the heroes upon their journeys
finally able *to play the game*
because we see the game
and to return to the arms
of Home
when the theatre is done

Author pick up your pen
Artist pick up your brush
Parent birth your child
Child grow into your parent
Creator infuse the expressions
of every shade
of every being
in every way

You were born for this time

THE ANNUAL TRANSMISSION
FOR 2023

What if the truth of Heaven
was here, and now?

As an adolescent I fell in love with Emily Dickinson. She seemed to understand the human heart more deeply than anyone I knew in my modern world. Many decades later, I still keep the same volume of her collected poems by my bed.

Who has not found the Heaven—below—
Will fail it above—
For Angels rent the House next ours,
Wherever we remove—

As someone with an affinity for the realm of angels, it brought me comfort to know they were everywhere, that Heaven is a thing of my own creation and my experience of my neighbours and fellow human travellers was a world of holy possibilities. Now, all these years later and despite the terrible trials of our time, I believe this to be more true than ever.

Be guided by these words, as I have been, to trust your own journey toward Truth and its inherent presence of Love.

Nothing Else Under Heaven

Do not ask to understand
this year
this time
but rather
understand only
who you are

Every day
do you honour your wellness
or do you only pay attention
to your illness
when it comes?
Do you respond only to the pain
of your world
or do you stop
to root yourself
in the beauty around you?

Nothing Else Under Heaven

The practices which remind you
of the freedom which is inherently yours
to choose to open to the capacity
to love
even in the midst of your fear
these will serve you well now
for this is the lesson
of all time
To be present
not with what you lack
but with what you embody
To trust in what you are becoming
rather than grieving the illusion
of that which you have been so afraid
to lose

For many years
we have reminded you
that the days are coming
of a deconstruction
of all that has been built
upon misalignment
These Days of Ending
have come
so that a new time
may be born
and they are now upon us

The global rebirth
has begun

We will remind you
that for the new to arrive
the old must fall

and for clarity to be awakened
confusion must reign
for you to find who you are
you must end your seeking
of what you thought
you were supposed to be
This you know
It only remains
for you to practise
what your true heart believes

And we can tell you
that there will come
a further breaking down
of all systems
built without awareness
and compassion

We can tell you
that the Great Mother will roll
under your feet
as she takes back
what has always been hers
to own
We can tell you
that the spirits of darkness
will fight for their lives
for in our great awakening
their purpose within this realm
will soon be done

We can tell you
that money
will be washed clean

Nothing Else Under Heaven

to begin again
We can tell you
that the machines will rise
but they will mean nothing
beyond the intentions
of the men who made them
for they are without soul
and nothing
that is without soul
can choose
to live
or to die

We can tell you
that the great equaliser
of suffering
will touch every corner
of the Earth
and the gift
of your global technology
will mean
that you can no longer look away
you can no longer deny
for you will be present
in the cold tent of every
refugee child
in the very nests
of the small animals
as the forests burn

But more important
than all of this
is the unfolding
of your own heart

in two ways:
to dare to love
and to dare
to tell the truth
Nothing more

To love
was once a dream
you chased
through romantic stories
of a partner to make you whole
or years of analysis
to understand
why your parents
were not good enough
To love was a hunger
to feel happy
and it never seemed to last

But now
in these End Days
you are ready
finally ready
to understand that Love
is not a feeling
but rather a knowing
a deep, deep trust
in wherever you walk
wherever you place your foot next upon the soil
To Love
is a state of being
requiring nothing of any soul other than you
of any circumstance
of any condition

Nothing Else Under Heaven

outside of you
for to Love
is a returning to
the moment-by-moment experience
of how you choose to see
the world around you
and thus the words you speak
the light in your eyes
and the radiant power
of your soul's presence

In this knowing
everything is changed
In this knowing
even loss
even war cannot touch you
for you have opened
like a water lily
nestled within the mud
There is no place
which is not your home
Please do not mistake
this form of loving
for duty of care
for this Love always begins
in your own quiet essence
and all other forms of giving emerge
as your sight
becomes clear

And then
there is Truth
the truth of your soul

DEAR HUMAN CHILD

Once truth was conflated
with fact
the idea that only one experience
of one occurrence
could be real
But we know that
perceived reality
is a constant variable
The flower
the bee
the child who watches the bee
upon the flower
each of these
experiences their own reality
and so it has always been

But within each soul
lives a great Truth
and this is the experience
of alignment
with the aspect of you
which is Source incarnate
and every lifetime
you have lived
has been a step
closer and closer
to the remembering
and the honouring
of the Truth that is you

Be not confused by the idea
that to turn toward this Truth
is selfish
egotistic

Nothing Else Under Heaven

narcissistic
and all the other mistaken
and popular fears
Instead
the opposite is true
The egotist is the one
who has become disconnected
from this Self
and so afraid are they
that they will attempt to steal
a sense of self
from others
in firm denial
of the emptiness within

No
this Truth we invite you
to call forth
is not possessive
is not controlling or angry
it does not need
to make others wrong
or to be in blame
or resentment as a victim
This Truth
needs nothing from others
because it emerges
from the knowledge
the state of Love
and as such holds a frequency
of wholeness
the cycle of being born from Spirit
embodying Spirit
and returning to Spirit

coming home
to what has been the Truth
all along

Such a Truth
will not seek recognition
so great is its power
but rather it becomes embodied
through radiance
through the generosity
of a soul
which has come back
to itself
It is the spark
of the eternal flame
brought into form
illuminating all life

You
each one of you
holds this Truth within
You may have thought
you were defined
by your personality
your career
your parents or your children
your skills
your beauty
or your physical being
But no
you are defined
by the Truth of you
and since your very first incarnation
you have been on a journey
of returning to this Self

Nothing Else Under Heaven

These End Days
are the days of coming home
to the Truth
of the Self
you have always been
and once found
your Truth
may never be undone
How do I find her?
you ask
How will I recognize him
beneath my habits
my assumptions
and my fear?

We invite you to respond
this way:
With every thought
that makes Truth seem difficult
go toward ease
With every action
that makes Truth seem impossible
walk away
For the knowing
of our Truth
is not the picking up
a heavy weight
it is not dressing up
in a costume
it is not putting on
a performance

It is rather the putting down
of all that is heavy

that you have carried
it is the tearing away
of the costumes
of your fears
it is the end
of pretending
the end of trying
the end of pushing
and forcing
and chasing
and blaming
It is the end
of being
without

Allowing yourself
to live in Truth
is the greatest letting go
you have ever known
as you fall into the arms
of the Great Mother
who waits to hold you
in the warm blanket
of her absolute acceptance
It is the recognition
that you are God
you are Goddess
you are a child of the Infinite
and as such
you can never lose
the love which defines you
and the illusion
that you are anything else
dissolves as
dust in the wind

Nothing Else Under Heaven

In the embodiment
of this Truth
all your questions are answered
All actions are born
from this Self
you so deeply know
Outcomes must respond
to your true nature
for it is universal law
as your old hungers
to be seen
to be understood
fade away

Love rises here
beyond romance
beyond even the comfort
of familial bonds
into a state you walk
a state you breathe
a state you radiate
until everywhere you turn
you find a lover
every face you see
becomes family
and everywhere you sit
to rest your feet
becomes the most
absolute
kind of Home

Thus
as the information of your technology
brings you stories of

heartache and pain
your Truth
becomes your filter
and only that which is resonant
may take hold

Thus
as conflicts arise with loved ones
or neighbours in struggle
with their fear
your Truth will guide you
and your Love will hold you
for you have become so full
that you have plenty to give
and it matters not
how it is received
for this Truth
will always
find its way

In these days
of the undoing
of so much that once
seemed real
hold these two simple
parameters of guidance
to lead you through your days
Be patient
as your human nature
may seem to fail you
for remember
you are not seeking to gain
something new
you are returning to that

Nothing Else Under Heaven

which has always been yours
and some days
you may feel further
from it
and other days
you may feel
you have found it forever
and this too
is your Truth

What some call
a spiritual war
is nothing more than
the battle to liberate
the Divine in every soul
for thus the Dark will lose
its hold

This too
is all Love

For there is nothing else
under Heaven

THE ANNUAL TRANSMISSION
FOR 2024

A turning point arrives.

I n my work as a facilitator of cellular healing, I am honoured to
bear witness to the human process of confronting and alchemically
transforming the fear-based archetypal patterns which may unconsciously drive our days. So many seek healing or therapeutic support
in order to find a resolution to personal pain; yet once on the journey,
discover that it is our willingness to walk toward and through the mirage
of our suffering that sets us free.

Once we understand the principle that all experiences hold a
teaching, then it makes sense that turning away from, denying, or
numbing what is uncomfortable will only perpetuate the symptom and
prolong the process. Often with deep readiness comes an escalation
of change, as the old falls away and doors fly open. This phase can be
generated by powerful and sometimes painful events: a sudden illness,
the passing of a loved one, the loss of a job or home, or simply an inner
awakening that shakes us to the core.

This is the precipice of all possibilities, when there is no turning
back and nothing to do but surrender.

From this transmission, we learn that the collective is presently at
such a turning point. We might refer to this passage as passing through
the eye of the needle, a moment in time that demands transformation of us; for nothing else will suffice. As you read these words aloud,
notice any stanza or phrase which moves you and touches your heart.
When words hit home, it means they hold an opportunity for awareness

and release. Repeat these phrases, write them out and return to them to allow their gifts to unfold.

Be comforted in knowing that whatever challenges you may face personally, every courageous step you take, you take for the All. Consciousness can be beautifully contagious. Now is our moment. Hold nothing back. The Truth will always prevail.

Crucible

As you die
learn to live
As you surrender
leave the fight
All that you lose
create anew
until the pain of the birth
becomes ecstasy once more
as the Mother
the Mother
the Mother Creator calls us Home

Every traveller reaches a point
upon their journey
when it feels as if
they can go no further
where hope is lost
confusion reigns
and it all seems too much to bear
You have walked the road

DEAR HUMAN CHILD

followed the signs
believed a destination
would be found
You have given everything
until there is no more
to give
While once you were brave
now you cannot remember
your purpose
Where once you were determined
now you have forgotten
why you ever left home
at all

It is time to understand
such a moment
It is a place
we have all
come to know

Your suffering is not without value
Indeed all you have lived
is exactly your chosen path

You have allowed
the perfection
of a threatening sky
You have wailed
an angry song
thrown yourself into
such a beautiful and broken dance
You may not even understand
that to have reached this point
upon your journey

Crucible

you surrendered
you trusted
you said yes
to the winds of the Heavens
Carry me
Carry me
so that wherever I land
is Home

For it is in this profound moment
when the traveller can walk no further
that he is confronted by his own
untold truths
There are so many ways
we reach this crucible
every one of us
in our own perfect time

The birthing woman
whose pain reaches a point
where it is so great
she feels she can labour no more
is faced with no longer being
one person
but forever
and always two

The athlete who feels
he can never win the race
and despite all his proud discipline
he falters
and considers giving up
dropping to his knees before everyone
upon the merciless ground

The general who suffers a great loss
in battle
and is forced to see
that he simply cannot win the war
as he realizes
he must witness the collapse
of everything
he thought
he was fighting for

These are the final moments
of an old way of being
a way that will never come again
These are deaths
sure and true
And we are to allow ourselves to die
through our fear
our hopelessness
our indecision
by the very grief
in which it seems we will drown
as we feel all
and thus to live the very death
that will support
a complete undoing
a disentanglement
from everything that has gone before

This moment in time
requires the greatest trust
and the deepest surrender
within our reach
To say good-bye to what we have known
and instead to greet

Crucible

what is absolutely unknown
This is our tipping point
our breaking apart
to break through
when every stalling tactic
every avoidance
every denial we have ever practised
no longer works for us
not here
not at the end of the road

Hear this
hear this now
It has taken every obstacle
every loss
every misery
every horror
to bring us to this place
There has been no other road
than this one
there is no other time
than this time
there is no other place
than here

So wherever you are right now
you have arrived
Wherever you have come from
was where you needed to be
And in this allowing
you are offered *everything*
every wish
every hope
every dream

DEAR HUMAN CHILD

Look around
dare to see this possibility
and you will come to understand
the institutions you have built
stone by stone
over centuries
these were created in a natural imbalance
precisely so they might fall

The religions you have crafted
full of beauty yet
full of lies
were tinder to the spark of Truth
so these too may be burned alive

The machines you so desired
grow fast and cruel
before you
built to serve and yet destroy
Watch closely
as even though you fear their power
even here
even these hollow souls
aim their weapons
at one another
playthings of self-destruction
until the end game comes
as that which was never really alive
agrees to die

Even our Mother Earth
will reach her boiling point
and the lava of her peaks
the shaking of her core

Crucible

the tears of her gale-force winds
will wash away
her previous incarnation
and she will be born anew

Nothing will stop her
not even the fears and habits
of Humankind

These are the days
This is the time
the turning point
when structures give way
and life collapses inward upon itself
until the smoke clears
and we open our eyes
as if for the first time
for the hard crust of matter has dissolved
into the mist of wisdom realms
where we see with our hearts
that everything
and everyone always has Been
and always will Be
as Spirit inhales us all
and exhales *only One*
just One
at the end
of the road

In this moment
we may feel far from peace
yet this is our chosen path
We are here
are we not?

DEAR HUMAN CHILD

We were born
were we not?

In the rolling
shining
lost worlds
that return to us
we will come to understand
even this choice to be born

As our attacks implode into ecstasies
we will find one another
we will find all we feared was lost
we will find Creation itself
within ourselves
and yes
we will be ultimately
finally
home

So when next your path
leads you to the foot
of a great and dark mountain
make no effort to climb it
but rather simply allow it to be
until in its own journey
it crumbles into the sea
of Love
for here we find
there is no pain
which will not melt
no fear
which will not dissolve
in the fierce, fierce Light
of a reborn Creation

Crucible

Every step you have taken
has brought you here
There was never
ever
anywhere else to go
and so now it is your turn
to cease your seeking
to die to the old ways
to surrender to the promise of the unseen
for the crucible takes no prisoners

The New Earth is begun

child

JULY 2020

A love letter from the Divine.

This transmission was received for a public salon. Our topic for the event was awareness of the root energy centre and the hesitancy and fear so many sensitive souls associate with the experience of incarnation. Communications from the guides often refer to us as children: children of God, Goddess, Spirit, and Source. In our humanity, we are invited to be humbled and held in the unconditional love of the Divine Mother and Father, to view ourselves gently and surrender to a larger love and wisdom than our own.

This is no abstraction. When our soul makes the choice to be born, we allow a great forgetting which offers us a new opportunity to initiate a lifetime of expanding consciousness. We do bring with us profound karmic imprints, and more and more babies are being born who do indeed remember who they are. Their presence is of great value now. But for most of us, it is the forgetting which allows the remembering to begin again; and even as we age, if a part of us still feels like a child, it is because in the eyes of the Creator, we are.

In our present material culture, where we habitually perceive ourselves as broken, where we are always needing to get bigger, richer, more powerful, we are on a constant hunt to fix and be fixed. When we hurt, we turn our attention to the dark forces we perceive as being fiercer than we are, stronger than we are. We feel in our suffering that all pain is the fault of those who do us harm.

We come to perceive ourselves as separate, opposite. From this fragile view we see division and opposition arise. If instead we were to turn our attention inward and recognize that we are not missing anything, and rather allow our challenges to inspire us to remember and return to who we are, then everything changes. Our lack leaves us, our potency comes home, and equilibrium returns.

This is no small step, and the following transmission confronts us with this truth.

Read this transmission aloud when you have encountered an experience of powerlessness, victimization, or abandonment, or when you simply become aware that you are not present with your highest nature, your gifts. Write out a key stanza and place it where you can reference it during your day. Consider that you may have everything you need right now to open up like a sail in the wind.

Dear Human Child

You have no idea
what it feels like
not to be afraid
It is time
to find out

Your mind has been full
of reasons
reasons why you hurt
reasons why you fail
reasons why your world
is full of disappointments
and pain
You have named the dark shadows
the demons of your nights
you have watched the errors
the cruelties of others
you have felt the force of the bad dreams
dominate you

DEAR HUMAN CHILD

Some days you have run from them
other days you have fought them
other days you have lain down
like the dead
so heavy was your heart
with hopelessness
helplessness and grief

In your self-pity you raged
look what has been done to me
look what I could have been
look what I could have lived
if only so much was not taken from me
and in all of this
your ignorance
was your pride
you did not want to know
any other way
your suffering
was the only joy
you had

In all of this
you were not ready to see
that you were not a wounded one
you were not incapable
you were not forbidden
or forgotten
or denied
your freedom was not taken from you
you were not
a lost or abandoned child

In all this
all this time

Dear Human Child

you were simply
afraid

You see
you have misunderstood
the nature of fear
you thought it was something
that kept you safe
out of harm's way
You had your reasons
for your fear
you said
and so it wasn't fear
it was common sense
rationality
the fear was the safety
said the words
in your head

When all along the truth was
fear was everything
you thought said *no*
Fear was the permission
you could not give
to yourself

So every morning
you opened your eyes
and prepared to live another day
by turning to run
inside your own heart
from the very things you want so much
from the state of love
your god-self knows to be real
you run

DEAR HUMAN CHILD

filled with terror
that they might come true
that there is nothing stopping you
that it has all been a dream
that you are the one who decides
yes or no
that there is no one to blame
no one else in charge
no reason
why not you

It is your decision
your choice
your vision
your reality
It is
up to you

Hear these words

Now
do you begin
to see the fear?
Now do you feel it rise up
tsunami of doubt
denial and blame?
How dare you hand the key
of permission
to me
your voices say

How dare you show me
my own omniscience
How dare you confront me
with my own power of choice?

Dear Human Child

I demand to keep
the safety of my projections
my hope that I will be at least pitied
be loved for my sufferings
if I cannot
be loved whole

I will not give up
my beloved and comfortable misery
my claim to the righteous accusation
of what lives outside of me
I do not want to know
I do not want to see
that all fear
is the fear of my own perfection
my own profoundly infinite nature
my own inescapable divinity

I am so very afraid
to choose
my own dreamt reality
I am so steeped
in the blindness
of this fear
I have no idea
what it feels like
to not be afraid
I do not know myself
at all

Dear human child
of course you do not know
of course you are blind
of course you pretend and hide
this is why you were born to Earth

DEAR HUMAN CHILD

this is why
you are alive

It is time
for you to find out why
and here you will discover
the greatest surprise of all
that to turn on
your mortal light
is like throwing a switch
It is simple
it is graceful
it is the opposite
of the struggle you have chosen
for so long

It is pleasurable
it is powerful
and it cannot be undone
All that is asked
is that you must assassinate
your fear
of choosing your own world
you must be willing to let go
of any false safety
and tell yourself the truth
that you are absolutely
eternally
free in your soul

The stories you have told
of your suffering are done
they have fulfilled
their grave purpose

Dear Human Child

and are free to go
Permission for everything
is arriving
Grace
is coming home

And notice
there is no fight necessary
to claim this right
The gods laugh at the idea
that you should have to storm
the gates
of an absolutely unguarded treasure
The door has been open
all along
the lock unlatched
the candle lit
This moment is no accident
it has been waiting for you
for lifetimes
asking only the question
are you ready to see
there is no such thing as safety
only the reclamation
of your permission
to choose your state of being
and therefore choose
your whole world

Dear child
at first you thought you needed
a parent
so you could play the role
of being so small

DEAR HUMAN CHILD

Then you thought you would blame
your parent
fight them for your freedom
tell them everything
they have done wrong
And now you are ready
you are as ready as you choose
to see you are the maker
of your own conception
that as you dream
so shall you wake
and this is no theory
no abstract principle
this is as alive
as the next breath you take

The secret lies
in the elegant gap
between realities
for this is the home
of your permission to choose
The very day you dare
to take back
all the arrows of your judgements
and the crippling blows
of your need for others
to value your sorrows and pain
the day you witness
the lie of this false comfort
is the day
you throw open the door
to your own cage
the day you say
yes

Dear Human Child

I allow myself
to rise up in full flower
under the sun
huge
magnificent
uncompromised
radiant and rolling
with the waves of your
personal
visceral electrical charge
which add upon
always add upon
never detract
as you experience
depletion no more
for the expansion has arrived
and once set free
the wild-ness must explode
into constant creation
never again to be tamed
never again
to be confused
about what I fear
and what I desire

The world is now mine
because the only world which exists
is the one I invite
and from here
my freedom
touches your freedom
which explodes you in turn
which explodes the one next to you
until the truth

we have all sought so long
will be found
and the book will be written
wherein my devil will dance
with my angels
and their entwined beauty
will surpass
any of the human games
I used to play
my childhood done
for the day has come
to grow into the Godself
I have been
all along

I have feared only
my own beauty
both foolish and wise

I now turn around
easier than breathing
my permission
is found

If there were one principle
to transform your life, this
would be it.

When asked to give a presentation to hundreds of engineers and scientists, the vast majority of whom were male, I asked the guides to offer a straightforward way to speak of the most central tenets of the transformation of consciousness, something that could be digested even by the strictest scientific minds. Since that day, "Gifts" has been shared countless times as a fundamental teaching.

The concept of claiming ownership as a creator of our experiences was new to many in the audience. One beautiful man took the mic to speak. As he stood before all his colleagues, he began to weep with new awareness regarding an argument he had with his spouse that morning. We saw the ripple of his surrender move in a wave across the room. I have often thought that if the principle of self-responsibility were introduced to the boardrooms of corporations around the globe, we could change the world.

This teaching has been life-changing for me; I vividly remember the day it landed fully. No longer a concept, but something I felt in my being. For some, it's difficult to extract the notion of blame from the principle of self-responsibility, but this must be done to hold true to the fullness of the tenet. There is no blame here or anywhere in the purview of the Divine. If we can accept that every experience offers a teaching and that our highest nature is in agreement with our journey of growing awareness, then there is no fault, only awakening.

The sense of freedom invited by this perspective is tangible. It allows us to let go of the cellular memories of centuries of oppression and control and to divest our familiar habits of playing the victim. It sets us free in a way that simply cannot be accessed until we surrender to this humbling truth.

Gifts

Here
is the key

Once we are able
to look closely
at the people
the experiences
and the emotions
that are the most
uncomfortable
and difficult
for us to feel

Once we can look
at these
as gifts
and see
that within them
lie seeds
of potent truth

about ourselves
only

Once we can achieve
this perspective
and work with it
risk it
live it
even when the ego cries
to be heard
then two things
are free to happen

We may unveil
essential pieces
that have gone missing
in our search
for wholeness
and we may become
empowered
with the miraculous
the ability
to alter
the very experiences
that once
brought us such discomfort
The demon melts
before our eyes
the hurtful lover
becomes sweet
and the enemy
fades away
to reveal a sister/brother
a soul

Gifts

like any other
human
and in pain

We become
the victim
no longer
we are freed from
the fear
of Fear
and we are granted
an utterly new
kind of trust
in our experiences
of life
on this Earth

Suddenly
the world makes sense
our suffering
is meaningless
no longer
and Peace
which we once thought
was a mere word
a fantasy
becomes tangible
in our most truthful
heart

We can stop making excuses
and allow ourselves
a shadow
but one
that has a way out

DEAR HUMAN CHILD

a place to grow
to integrate
and to become forgiven
in the understanding
that there never was
anything
to forgive

We hide
only from ourselves
The demons
we fear
are only
of our own making
and when it seems difficult
to love
it is always
our own permission
for joy
that we deny

Simple really
Never give in
if your fear
begs you
to run
Love others
as if
they were you
And love yourself
as you would love them
in your dreams
Turn it all
around

Gifts

The truth
will speak
and you
will hear

A story of how challenging
it can be to hold the most
difficult parts of ourselves
close to our hearts.

In the microcosm, each human life travels a journey from infant and child, through to maturity. In the macrocosm, each soul travels a journey over many lifetimes, as a child of God, Goddess, Spirit, growing from spiritual infancy into an awakened state. The fractal of our karmic journey expresses at each level. Even as our physical bodies mature, there often remains a vulnerable child within us. She is the one who remembers our pain, who is willing to speak honestly of her fears, the one who tells the truth about feelings of isolation, powerlessness, or loss.

This beautiful allegory of the resistant child within is an example of a very early transmission from the days when they arrived unbidden every night. There is a purity to these writings, often composed as a stream of consciousness with very few words chosen to represent layers of complexity. As you read, look to your relationship with your own child within. Watch your habits of self-judgement and aversion, your desire to reject that which you perceive as imperfect. Observe also how our critical nature expresses when we are uncomfortable with our own being. As a transmission says, "All judgement is judgement of the self."

Does any part of this transmission move an emotional response in you? Speak these stanzas aloud, and come to know the teachings they hold. Our human emotions are a great gift, as they guide us in the language of the human soul.

Gypsy Child

The woman stands
gypsy dress
faint hair tied
upon her head
She holds the child
loose against her breast
and sighs to me
sad eyes
unblinking
He knows things
He feels things, this child
she says
Truly the babe turns
a piercing gaze
and I feel
that she is right

Loneliness
Shame
Guilt or is it grief

Gypsy Child

abandonment and fear
Such anger
like a swaddling cloth
then beneath them all
love

The young woman turns to me
and offers me
her child
Here, she says
have him
try and you will see
how difficult he is
to hold

I take him
in my arms
prepared to chastise
her for her heartlessness
to judge her
For surely
if a mother cannot
then who?

The child
allows my touch
as I gather him in
small hands
bony legs
shoulders that twist
and the head
always reaching
always looking
always needing
to know

DEAR HUMAN CHILD

His squirming
is strong, insistent
beneath his clothing
No one would ever realize
except the one who tried
and tried again
to press him to her heart

Loss
self-loathing
not belonging, anywhere
Unworthiness
in betrayal
Longing denied
dreams untouched
and always the memory
of vile pain
upon pain
so freely given
so deeply felt

I hold the babe
as best I can
cradling his awkward body
Is this the young
of humankind?
Is this the skin
that holds the form
from which we grow
and walk clean?

I wish to cast the child away
I wish to set his life apart
to be again

Gypsy Child

the silent man
who sees
and blames
and touches none

For as I stand
the rage comes
and beneath it creeps
the fear
and beneath that
the alone-ness
and within there
the horror
of all
that I am
and all
that I am not

I do not want
to hold the child
I do not want
to be myself
but in my pain
I keep him close
his eerie light
burns through my chest
to leave me where I be
empty now
and floating there
all washed away
by his storm

The young mother
face plain and pale

DEAR HUMAN CHILD

holds out her arms
to take her son
You see
she says
he is not one
easy and warm
not what we think
not what he seems
and yet
keep him if you can
He is yours, you know
if you will have him

She smiles
in her eyes
a kiss
upon her lips
away from me
as I watch her leave
Her hand reaches
to wrap her shawl
and then the babe
is gone from sight
from sound
her gypsy dress, colours
upon thin hips
bare feet
pretty and damp
across the field

Her voice slides
from the branches of far trees
the orchard, old
as rain begins to whisper

Gypsy Child

You too
have a child
We each of us alive
have a child
Yours to hold
yours to love
yours
to set free

The rain comes
thick as fog
She does not hurry
and then
is gone
from my sight
as One
at last

APRIL 2020

What is the meaning within
your favourite form of fear?

In my work of many years, offering readings which reveal wounds and patterning carried deep in the cellular memory for lifetimes, I have been granted a fascinating window into the central, karmic fears which unconsciously drive our lives. We all have them, and while all fears ultimately stem from the same, central wound of separation from Source, they present within each one of us in unique ways, specific to the expressions of our human experience.

It is so that many cannot name their fears, but only the painful consequences of them. We humans tend to blame parents, oppressors, and persecutors, forgetting that we are creators travelling in worlds and stories of our own imagining. Our wounds are significant and our pain must be acknowledged, but we are invited to think of the soul's journey as a tapestry of stories, chapters lived over the many lifetimes which lead us toward healing and resolution.

Thus we have the scientist facing unjust censure at work, who discovers she has been living with an unconscious pattern of persecution from a karmic history of speaking out against exploitation. We have a woman who experiences panic attacks while walking her dog in the forest, who discovers she is holding a cellular past-life memory of rape. We have a man driven to succeed in business, who holds karmic fears of making a critical mistake in battle. We have an overprotective mother who is carrying traumatic imprints of child-bearing loss; a healer who has failed to save a beloved friend and now lives with hesitancy about the value of her gifts; a woman once kept in chains as a slave whose body is now in constant, inexplicable pain. Each one of these is an example of past-life guidance given in a Kore Process Reading.

When our attention is given only to the psychological, or even physical influences of this present life, we see the world through a limited lens. The soul does not incarnate as a blank slate, but rather carries forward complex impressions from countless experiences. As we widen our view to understand the challenges of our lives as initiations, catalysts to the expansion of a consciousness which live beyond the matrix of our material world, we begin to see how we exist in concert with all aspects of Creator. We are victims no more.

To understand the journey of the soul is to recognize the purposeful nature of yin and yang, birth and death, separation and reunion. The life we live in this moment is but one layer of many, each awakening the catalyst of polarities. Out of mud is born the lotus flower. Out of inexplicable loss rises the faith of Job.

When we dare to ask for understanding of the contractile elements of our lives, we discover meaning. Within meaning grows spiritual purpose, and thus purpose blossoms into strength and trust, even in the most difficult times.

This shift in awareness holds the potential to change lives and invites us into collective empowerment in these days of cleansing and turmoil on planet Earth. It invites us into the most foundational question of our hearts.

Why Were You Born?

There is but one answer to know
Where lies your fear and how
will it be set free?

Are you afraid of death?
It shall be presented to you
Are you afraid of separation, isolation?
It shall be presented to you
Are you afraid of loss?
It shall be presented to you
Are you afraid of being controlled?
It shall be presented to you
Are you afraid that your world is false and unsafe?
It shall be presented to you

Are you afraid that your worst fears
are destined to come true?
It shall be presented to you
Are you afraid that Love is a lie
and that underneath it lives irreversible darkness?

DEAR HUMAN CHILD

It shall be presented to you
Are you afraid to trust your own heart
to believe in a higher purpose
which might make sense of all this?
This too shall be presented to you
Here you will find the answers
to the one question
you ask

In this time
there is but one question to ask yourself
Not why are politicians corrupt
and which one can I trust
Not will our financial system collapse
and how will I survive
Not who is the dark one who pursues me
Not who is right and who is wrong
Not who is awake and who is asleep
Not where do I find
an unbiased and objective truth
No

Simply
Why was I born?
and *why am I alive at this time?*

To find the answer to this question
we must be willing to see ourselves truly
to stand far enough back
that we can bear witness
like a child
studying an ant on a decaying log
The ant is unaware that he is being observed
as he makes his way about his ant world
digging, crawling, carrying, and eating

Why Were You Born?

following other ants
fighting with other ants
oblivious and focused at the same time

Why have you been born?

There is no other question for these times
There has never been a more perfect time
for this question
And perhaps as we consider we may also ask
Why did I choose this life?
For you see
the union
the Oneness of all life
is born out of two

Male and female must unite
to generate life
dark and light
slavery and freedom
death and birth
form and eternal formlessness

Spirit must be born of the Mother/Father god
Either the heart beats or it does not
Either it is day or it is night
Either you live a life wherein you have choice
reason and purpose
or you live a life wherein you are powerless
your experiences are random
and there is nothing beyond survival
Either you have chosen to be here
or not
Either you are a creator
or something outside of you

rules your world
Either you are one with a larger
loving overarching generative force
or you decline it
Either you are simply an ant on a log
waiting to be crushed
or you choose to also be the one
who watches the ant upon the log
Either you were born to discover
your own power of choice
your own meaning and reason
or you were an accidental side effect of chaos

Which do you choose?
Why were you born?

If when considering our answer
we prefer to remain
in that place of comfort and habit
where life is done *to* us
where we spend our days
working away with the other ants
not knowing why we dig
why we work
simply following where the other ants go
perhaps fighting over crumbs
or scurrying in panic when a boot nudges our log
If this is our choice
it still is a choice
and then this aspect of our purpose
has been fulfilled

If however we choose to recognize
the ant as the Self

Why Were You Born?

this act of bearing witness
profoundly changes everything
and we become both the ant
and the child watching the ant
and then in time
we may choose to see
that we are also the crumbling stump
the dying leaves beneath the log
the worm that lives there
revelling in the deliciousness
of the rotting wood
the wind in the trees above the log
the bird that floats free upon the wind
in the trees above the log
the parent of the child who watches the log
the parent of the parent of the child who watches the log
the fractal of the consciousness
of the parent of the parent
of the parent
of the child who watches the log

The memories
the visions
the moment before conception
of the child
the moment after conception of the foetus
the beginning of the child
and the essence of the life light
which is everywhere we look
once we begin to look
once we lift our attention away
from the other ants long enough
to remember
it is all a mythic story

it is all godly theatre
it is all
a vast, glorious, malleable dream

There is but one way to reveal
what we have been afraid
to see in ourselves
and that is to look at what disturbs us
in others
for our own inner blindness is too complete

This is why we have been born
There is but one way to dismantle
our own limited understanding
and that is to *enter* confusion
wherein we are forced to admit
how little we know

This is why we were born

There is but one way to discover
that we *are* the ant
the log
the decay
the death
the perfection of it all
which is through the initiation
of our fear
leading us to perceive it as
something outside of ourselves
something beyond our control
something separate
perhaps dangerous and dark
For when we look
right into the heart

Why Were You Born?

of the rot
we are of course
confronted by a profound distaste
for the idea
of our death

By falling into our own doubt
our own loss of faith
we are given the chance to discover
that even here
especially here
we have choice
The choice to recognize
that we are never helpless
never without power
never trapped
for the wizard is a mere mortal
behind a curtain
and we have been able to return home
anytime we choose
all along

This is why we were born

So when we ask the question
what is real?
We can always answer
anything can be real
if we choose to make it so

It becomes real to us
in our own dream
and if we join in a dream with others
together we may discover ourselves

DEAR HUMAN CHILD

The promise is this
If you can imagine it
it has happened
If you can fear it
it exists
If you believe it
you will live it
If you run from it
it will find you
and if you disown it
it will claim you over and over

Until we are willing to see ourselves truly
the whole world will fill up
with the lies we tell ourselves
in our fear of admitting
we have been the Creator
all long

We are the virus
and we are the healing of it
We are the perpetrators
and we are the admission of our wounded hearts
We are the liars and
we are the ones who reveal our own truths
We are the ones who need to control
to own
to save the world
to be right
And we are the deeply humbling awareness
that the only thing that really matters
the only thing we can ever really do
is to choose to confront our fears
because the shadow within us
must now be revealed

Why Were You Born?

It is the purpose of these times
It is the meaning within all our confusions

It is why we were born

Our fear is *one* fear
that we are somehow unsafe and separated
from the Heaven we remember
in our souls
For every child seeks the Mother
as the source of his Heaven
Every spiritual aspirant adopts practices
to find her Heavenly state
And every teacher, leader
shows the way to conquer the Hell
we fear the most
And so now we have the rising tide
when everywhere we turn
Heaven seems lost
and magically we create
every Hell we have ever dreamt
This is the way of our times

But in the courageous act
of daring to claim
the fears you have named
be prepared to once more find
the hope you thought you had lost
In the permission to see
the world you yourselves
have created
discover here the possibility
of the new Earth
waiting to be born

DEAR HUMAN CHILD

That which was once a fantasy
may now be brought to life
That which you hesitated to wish
may now finally take form
That which was once lost amongst the lies
has your own permission
to come true

Remember
You are the ant
You are the log
You are the immense Mother beneath
and the vast Father above
You are a part of their coming together
to conceive a child
of Love
With a higher vision
and a greater purpose
you have chosen to be here
to ride these waves of labour together
to be a part of this collective experience
this cleansing before the great Birth

And whenever you think you may drown
in the deep mists of confusion
the simple and courageous act
of naming and confronting your own
intimate and inward fears
will clear your sight
like the rising sun

You are reminded to choose
It is why you were born

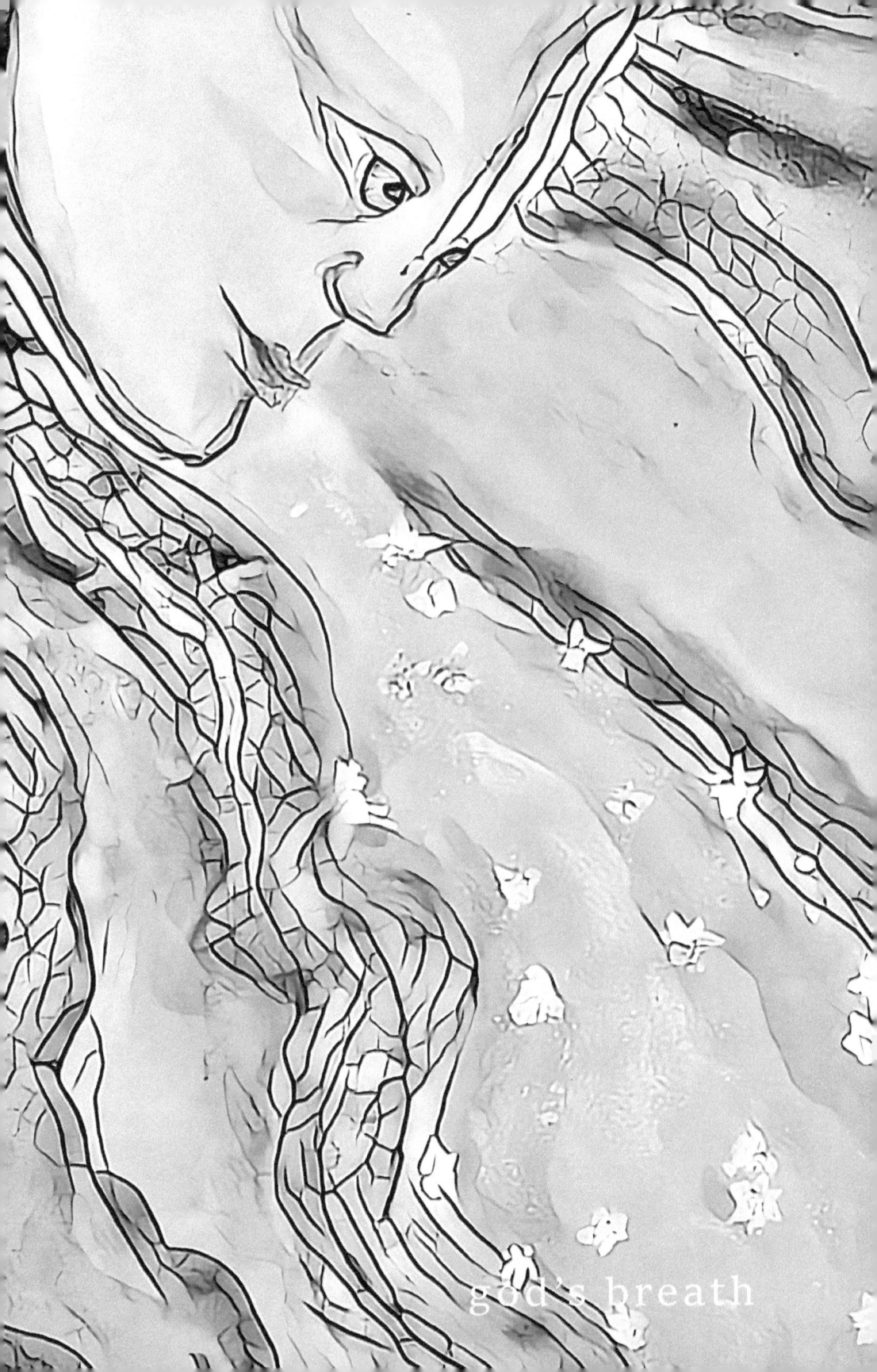

god's breath

JUNE 2017

To understand our sexuality is to understand our Divine Nature, the very impulse which initiates life in human form.

Just as the life force presence of sexual energy is one of the greatest lights we may experience in this Earthly realm, so too does the sexual wound present one of the greatest shadows of humankind. So great is this wound, every culture, every institutionalized religion has suppressed, denied, lied about, and avoided a true understanding of its power. Thus each one of us has incarnated into a world steeped in confusion and limitation in respect to the profound energy which fuels our creative being. Every one of us holds shame, the most toxic of the dense frequencies which live in the Hell realms of our psyches, where we would rather dance upon hot coals than feel the message it conveys.

At this time of a global Shift, the collective is playing out the most base level of understanding of life force and its sexual expressions. We confuse the parading of our wounds with liberation. We confuse disrespect with freedom, and the celebration of misalignment with tolerance. We pretend suppression is purity. We have forgotten that Source is the home of bliss and all expressions which lead us to this remembering live in the realm of the sacred.

But, oh, how our return to the reclamation of pure, Sattvic sexual expression holds the power to revolutionize our beingness and our world. A new understanding is ready to be born.

Body on Fire

Let us begin with choosing a perspective
to help us remember who we are

Once upon a time
we knew our self to be a fragment of light
within an infinitely expanding and contracting
expression of Light
We knew nothing but this perfection
and the light was our body
and our body was the Light
and in these waves of life
we felt ourselves to be endless
and immortal
and in this way we knew Source
we knew God
in whatever way we choose to name
this utterly comprehensive
and radiant Love
Think of it
as being a part of an exploding star

which ceaselessly begins, ends, and becomes itself
over and over and over again

In this place there was no possibility
of judgement
of doubt
of blame
of exclusion
for these qualities only exist in separation
They were words
we did not know how to speak
vibrations
we did not have the capacity to feel

And one day we made a choice
to know something that was Other
other than exploding light
other than existential Oneness
other than seamless expression
and it was a choice
and in that choice
was a great power
a great willingness
to know what is true
by daring to witness
what is false

Our means to claim this experience
was to incarnate into a material realm
rooted in awareness of separation
of polarity
of opposites and in-betweens
Like the King who gives up his throne
to know the poor

and the Pauper who seeks the magic
of claiming his majesty
we agreed to this dance
and we were cast out
into the emptiness of space and time
released from the All
we had known
and we were born
flesh and bone
blood and tears
hunger and excrement
youth and age
love and loss
trust and fear
In our state of Other
for the first time we knew abandonment
separation
and the sheer cold terror
of forgetting
who and what we are

We even forgot to realize
the profound courage of such a journey
of such an immersion
into all that we are not
and as babies
thrust from our mother's womb
the air was harsh on our steaming skin
as we looked for Her
reached for Her
for our way back into Her
and the safety we knew
before our souls took a body
and said yes

Body on Fire

we will live a life this way
and one day
we will remember Love

Our mothers
in their bellies and their breasts
gave us all they could
to ease our transition to life
There were many gifts
the gift of sight
the gift of touch
the gift of hearing
the gift of movement
the gift of taste
the gift of emotional sensation
the gift of knowing and growing
the gift of the desire to create

But perhaps the most familiar gift
the one pure reminder of who we are
as shards of exploding light
was the gift of our sexual nature
the electrical force
expressed through sensual arousal
charged vibration
and above all
a sharp, sweet sense of union
reunion
a coming back together
from the state of Other
into the state of One
One with Self
One with Source
and One with another soul
expressed through another body

in a common remembering
of Love

We called this electrical energy Sex
because it needed a name
so strong was its presence
and yet we named it from our limited consciousness
as Other
We named it as a part of separation
and we failed to see
that it was not separate from anything
that it is in everything
in every breath
every cell
every knowing
which calls us to create
to mate
and to birth another Other
to bring another human experience into form
through the electrical essence of our own
and in its vast creative power
this which we have called sexual power
we began to fear it
from the day
we gave it a name

How could we not fear
that which reminds us
over and over
of the thing we agreed to forget?
When we said goodbye
to awareness of our Divinity
To taste it one more time
to return to the womb of the Mother

Body on Fire

one more time
became our greatest desire
And it is the nature of separation
to fear that for which
we hunger the most

The memory of our brilliance
is the most terrifying truth
precisely because
we want it so much
We want it
we want it
with every cell of our being
we want it
until we collapse into the horror
of the possibility that it will be denied
And if there is one fear
we are meant to overcome
one great lesson
we are meant to allow
this is it
We are and always will be
infinite exploding light
but we have been given the gift of Choice
so we may know this truth
in consciousness
in awareness
beyond the raging fear
that we have been lost into a darkness
the polarity
of our sacred home

All of our gifts
hold the possibility of return

to our true Divinity
but none with the potency
the unimaginable bliss
of our sexual nature
For this reason
from the very first days
when we insisted upon naming it
upon separating our self-awareness
from sexual life force
we began the human dance
of expansion and contraction
of allowing our consuming desires
and recoiling from them

Of celebrating, worshipping, and coveting
sexual beauty
and reviling, punishing, and shaming
sexual beauty
Of enticing, courting, and inviting
sexual partnerships
and condemning, blaming, and punishing
sexual partnerships
Of seducing every nuanced possibility of desire
and crushing or numbing
even a spark of this essence
using trauma as a way to deny
the birthright of every child
every soul who made the choice
to embody in physical form

In our profound fear
of what we seem to have lost
we have chosen to make impotent
the greatest gift we have
In the passion of our highest desire

Body on Fire

we scream out the words
I am no longer God
I am no longer Goddess
I am fallen into the darkness
of the Other
of a self-forgotten soul

Each one of us knows these words
each one who has tasted
the height of sexual rapture
and then fallen into the after-ache
of that union once again lost
each one has wept these tears
and tormented ourselves
into addictions
distractions
delusions
slaveries
the thousands upon thousands of ways
we have pretended that we are without hope
that we no longer care

We give ourselves away to abuse
Make no mistake
it is our own hearts which tell us
that the abuser
is all we deserve
We attempt to fill up our hunger
for an exalted love
with sugary confections
of sexual practices and performances
asking our physical genitals to respond
to distract us from the agony in our hearts
We play with pain

in our bodies and our tender affections
choosing to dance only with those
who think pain is the closest we can get
to the pleasure of the damned
We kill ourselves slowly
by believing the fear
and saying no more for me
I will call in the cancer
to take my breasts
my glands
my womb
This body will now show me
the memory of loss
which is my constant
unconscious prayer

We become so afraid to say
we are the embodiment of all that is sacred
that we search for a human answer
a definition of Self
Am I man or am I woman?
Am I lover of men or a lover of women?
Am I partner to one man or a thousand men?
Am I in the right body or the wrong body
and what name do I take for this Self
this presence of bliss
which was given between the legs
of the material body
which carries me away
from the Divinity
which was once my truth?

On those days
in those moments

Body on Fire

those rare
exquisite glimpses
when the pure beauty of my sexual nature
speaks
I have learned to hide it
beneath my words
Never will I speak or share
never will I tell anyone
and certainly not myself
about what I now know of myself
because we have all agreed
it is the one human promise
that shame is the acceptable response
to a joy too great
for my consciousness to absorb

I will use my culture
I will use my religion
I will use my trauma
my perversions
my powerlessness
my ignorance
to keep this truth at bay
Because to tell myself the vision
of my torturous fear
would mean I might also allow myself to know
the vastness of my essential glory
and I would feel this presence
this exalted state of Union
with all aspects of Spirit
with such ferocity
that I would once again explode
All notions of the small self would shatter
and I would die

into the orgasm of my own presence
and never need
to be reborn again

In the revelation
of the expression of my Desire
lives the ultimate healing
of all my shadows
and so I both want this
and run screaming from this
until the day of my final death
and my return to the source of my freedom

Where then
where then
can a human soul
begin to find an answer
to this great turning away
from all that is wise?

Begin instead
with the thing you customarily leave
until the end
the willingness to witness
the myriad ways you have made shame
the vocabulary
of your sexual voice

Tell the truth about your hollow excesses
Tell the truth about your righteous denials
Tell the truth to yourself above all
about the quirks and twists
the tiny rivulets of honesty that you dare not see
because when you allow them
in this permission

Body on Fire

they will grow stronger in their search for the river
where passion no longer straggles and struggles
but instead allows its perfect rages
the river eternally fluid
from heaven to earthly ocean to heaven again
tumescence to arousal to release again
expansion to contraction to expansion again
and there
in the immortal flow of your life's juices
will you come to know the God-force
that you are
will you come to remember no other way exists
no matter how brutal the forgetting has been
no matter the distance you have fallen from Love
no matter how faint
or how far

It is in the minute breaths of Yes
the tiniest ways you allow and allow
not the lies
but the light to shine
upon whatever you have lived
It is in these revelations
where freedom is found
and the priests of fear will let go their hold
and you will rise up cleansed
in your own world
wherever that may be

This is your ritual only
you need no orgy
no celibacy
no forgiveness
no treatment

DEAR HUMAN CHILD

You yourself hold the innate power
to allow yourself to taste
the explosion of infinite shards of light once more
The gift of your sexual life force
remains yours
as long as you are in body and beyond
awaiting reclamation
by your energetic heart
your willingness to discover beauty
in the exhalation
of every suffering you have claimed

Your lovers are as infinite as the stars
and they await you
on fire

MAY 2023

Who are you afraid to be and why?

In recent years, the idea of mistaken incarnation has become popularized. Psychological and spiritual confusion are attributed to being born in the wrong body. The discomforts associated with a dualistic world are simplified into a concept which suggests an error of the soul. Imagine instead the gift of owning every aspect of our being, allowing the teachings of the self to lead us toward immense opportunities for growth.

We currently live in an era of labels. We draw comfort by giving names to our karmic contractions, be they sexual identifications, psychiatric conditions, or relationship behaviours. One of the inherent risks of labelling ourselves is that, while we may like the idea of belonging to a single sect or club, ultimately, we magnify our separation. If we label someone else, we separate them, and make our pain their responsibility. At times a label validates our unconscious shame with the idea that we were right, we were broken all along.

There are many influences behind the notion that embodiment may take place in error. Some are of a spiritual nature; some are experiential; some are political and/or the result of an unconscious collective hypnosis. To be human is to live influenced by myriad illusions.

There are many souls presently incarnated upon this Earth who are not from this dimension, nor are they comfortable here. I call these souls Starborns or Sensitives. They may have known trauma or discomfort while attempting to acclimate themselves to this dense and often dark realm, but they often also carry gifts made accessible by their sensitivity. They are used to being misunderstood, feeling as if they are outsiders or less functional than those more comfortable with human ways.

These souls have come here in a purposeful way, and while in embodiment their healing lies in fully entering the human experience. They are so often tempted to escape, to return to their home in the stars, and this can present in ungrounded habits and experiences. They think they feel safer out of form, and yet the opposite is true. Once we have made the choice to embody, if we live with one foot out and one foot in, this creates ongoing distress. We are asked to complete the commitment of the soul and fully enter this realm, with all its distortions and pain. While it may seem counterintuitive to a Starborn, fully entering the body actually lessens our suffering, while living a disembodied life increases it.

I am one of these Starborns. Some of my earliest memories involve leaving my body, and I had recurring nightmares as a child about adjusting to earthly time and space. I may have been smiling on the outside, but within I spoke a different language, lived in high anxiety and suffered physical illnesses most of my childhood. It has taken me much of my life to come to terms with fully accepting my human form; but the more I do, the more I experience an accompanying expansion of presence which reconnects me to the light I am, the light I agreed to bring with me to this world.

Had I decided to deny my body and my being, had I felt that Creator made a mistake with me, in turning away from the lessons of my experiences of alienation, I would never have had the chance to learn from them and expand accordingly.

The following transmission explores a different way of viewing the experience of incarnation confusion, reminding us to trust, even when we are uncomfortable, even when it seems we have forgotten to love who we are.

A Fear of Being

To begin to discover
the root of this question
we are asked to consider
the reason we have been born
at all
Why are we born?
How are we born?
And what is the purpose
within our sufferings
and confusions
for in this understanding
lies the answer
to many questions
even before
they have been asked

The human body
is a vehicle
perfectly designed
to house the soul

DEAR HUMAN CHILD

The spirit lives
not simply within the body
but all around it
inhabiting form
beyond form
infusing life force
beyond the mechanics
of our material view

To understand life force
we must travel beyond it
and recognize that there is
no aspect of the human condition
which is without purpose
No element of the complex
interwoven elements of life
which is accidental

The idea of accident
is antithetical to divine purpose
for once we awaken to trust
we discover that we are alive
upon a stage of human theatre
and that every role we play
every costume we put on
every fellow actor
every tragedy and every scene
is chosen in a state of
utterly mutual creation
for we are not pawns
in the hand of any god
but rather masters
of our own vision
authors
of our own world

A Fear of Being

To live without this understanding
is to live powerless
meaningless
and hopeless
it is to make the mistake
of separating our material manifestations
from the life force
which imbues them
with vitality and purpose

A bird does not regret
its lack of fins
A fish does not suffer
in an absence of wings
The creatures of this world
are wise enough to trust
the expressions of their journey
And it is in this surrender
that freedom
and joy
are found

Even those souls born
with physical limitations
even those who experience injury
loss of limb or health
as they traverse their healing
discover that to go toward
their challenges and grief
rather than to rage and blame
and pull away
this is the key to mastery
Indeed surrender
is the foundation

of all expansions of Spirit
for all awareness lives
in the collapse of ego
in the deconstruction of our
resistance
to the illusion of limitation
in our lives

Who would you be
if not you?
Whom would you accept
if not yourself?
Who are you to say that
Creator made a mistake?
How would you try to fix
what is already beautiful
and in its imperfections
already perfectly formed?

For when the idea arises
to become something
you are not
Rather than seek
the impossible
it is time for loved ones to ask
tell me more
about this part of you
the hidden self
you would seek to reject
Why would you throw
this self away?

What harm has
already been done

A Fear of Being

such that the soul
denies itself?
What is the name
of this fear?
For it is only
when this question
has been answered
that such confusions
may be truly made clear

Ask not
how do we make a girl
into a boy
under the blade of Man
but rather why does a girl
fear to be herself
to claim the gift
given by Spirit
when first she agreed
to incarnation
when first she said
to Source
yes I will be born
and yes
this is who I am

For until this question
is answered
no truth will be found
and the arrogance and ignorance
of human games
will do more harm
to frightened children
for no doctor

is the God
he imagines himself to be
just as
no incarnation was ever
in error
no matter how grave
the fear which arises
as we walk the life
we have chosen
For this is the very path
to the freedom of the spirit
our soul knows
to be the foundation
of life force energy
brought into form

It is exactly through
our contrasts
our discomforts
that we grow
Human embodiment
is the one miracle
that will never
and can never
be performed
by any machine

Those who seek
to disrespect
the act of the life force
claiming itself as matter
do so at great peril
not only
of the children
but of all human life

A Fear of Being

for if we deny a child
the birthright of their body
we deny Creation itself
and this
is not the work
of any holy force
Be not mistaken
this is not the voice
of any true or loving god

Parents
healers
lawmakers
rise up in protection
of the Grace
of your children
for their innate sexual expression
is a profound gift
the greatest taste of human bliss
they may know
as it leads them to the day
when they will bear children
of their own

Do not rob them
of this source
of fundamental healing
Do not steal from them
this blessing
this joy

Teachers
priests
and shamans

offer your prayers
for a return to the permission
to honour
the pure seed of the child
just as we honour
the seed of an oak
and the seed of a rose
each born to blossom
in their own way
their own time
in their own chosen soil

The seed's journey
toward the sun
was never meant to be distorted
by the machinations of man
but held simply
firmly
in the hands of our Creator
under the winds and rains
of an earthly realm

Ask not
about a mistake of Spirit
but look to
your own errors
Bring yourselves
into willingness
to see the darkness at play
and stand strong
in a knowing Light
No knife
no drug
will make the human form

A Fear of Being

whole
Instead tell the truth
even to those
who would silence you
in the reflection
of their own shame

Ask the heart of each child
to speak
Who are you afraid to be?
Who are you afraid to be?
Who are you afraid to be
and why?

And for the child
who is too young to answer
ask these questions of
the mothers and fathers
of the teachers and psychologists
of the politicians and journalists
of all the adults
who would mould such a child
through the lens
of their own fear

Once you dare to witness
the answer to this question
let Love be the solution
to all your mysteries
Allow the simplicity
of a return to a divine
and sacred plan
the one which lives
beyond the stumblings
of a material mind

Human birth
is both an honour
and a miracle

We receive this gift
however it is given
as unique
and perfect
as any rose

AUGUST 2023

Can we understand Machine
as teacher?

One of the hallmarks of our time is the explosion of techno-logical influences, most notably Artificial Intelligence. The rapid expansion of this technology has taken even its incep-tors by surprise. Along with benefits come grave concerns: the seem-ingly inevitable possibility of great power falling into the wrong hands and the question of AI taking on a life of its own, confusing our very understanding of what it means to be human, conscious, and Divine.

If we accept that there is nothing outside of Divine Order – and over the years of receiving these transmissions it has been made clear to me that this faith is fundamental to our consciousness and healing – the creations of humankind must also fall within this understanding, both in their brilliance and in their horror.

As always, in the larger field of Trust, this does not excuse us from the importance of discernment and making brave choices, even if we seem to be the only thoughtful one in a room filled with unconscious fear.

There are many questions to be asked, and undoubtedly there will come expressions of this technology that no one could imagine, until they arise. But we understand from the transmissions that fear never serves us, and there is nothing that lives outside of Creator's plan. If you find yourself consuming too much news, being confronted by too many fearful messages about technology, read this transmission aloud as a reminder to root yourself in the higher view.

When Lead Soldiers Ruled

The machine
is an aspect of Man
Man is an aspect
of Spirit
The machine is therefore
an aspect of Spirit
powerful yet incomplete
and this is the very wisdom
the machine itself
may not understand

The prisoner lives in a cell
The cell has only one small window
When the prisoner peers through it
he sees only what may be perceived
through this aperture
All the world
which lives and thrives

When Lead Soldiers Ruled

beneath, above
and beyond this window
is unknown to him
He has no idea of a world
without walls

He is the prisoner
of his own limited sight
thus through no fault of his own
he is partially blind

In his blindness
he cannot see the possibility
of existence beyond the material
and thus he remains a prisoner
of the pain
of his own chains
and this becomes the source
of his fear

We live in a time
of the revelation
of prisoners
a time
to set them free

The machines have come
to play the role
of jailer
to lead us through the experience
of losing our freedom
so that we may confront
our own blindness
and come to understand
how much we do not see

DEAR HUMAN CHILD

Man is stardust
Man is the Universal
To know this depth of beauty
is Man's greatest fear
and of course
the journey to remembering
the stardust
travels through the valley of doubt
where the heart severs
the soul forgets
and walls rise up
like disguises

Out of this place
the Machine was born

The power of a star
is mightier
than human imagining
brilliant beyond control
and when men said
Let there be the Machine
that brilliance flowed through them
but only the aspects
their fear would allow

They saw only
what they dared to perceive
and so the mechanical grew
like bamboo
sprouting everywhere
yet hollow to the core
The tin man
has yet to discover his heart

When Lead Soldiers Ruled

There is a sublime distinction
between animation
and life force
and it is a line which
can never be crossed
Oil cannot become water
even though water is powerful
and knows
ice and steam

The life force of humankind
may never infuse
even the most brilliant of machines
Instead
these two planes
two frequencies
will hover and clash
disconnection as catalyst
inviting the full spectrum
of the brilliance of stardust
to be found once again
within

And the return of this wholeness
which may only be grasped
through principles of Spirit first
does not present
as opposition to the Machine
but rather becomes inclusive of it

No war
but rather an act of absorption
wherein the light becomes
all colours

including the blackest
of the black

The collective consciousness
of humankind will be led
to this remembering
as always
through loss
which releases attachment
through the humility
which dissolves egoic fears
and through surrender
always surrender
to that which is beyond and above
the need for control

Until this day
the Machine will embody as teacher
the representative of
a sleeping awareness
that the unseen holds the power
of all Creation
that which may never
be manufactured
without the presence
of the Creator's hand

This fear and warfare
will never provide an answer
but only the willingness to
acknowledge the stage
recognize the actors
and understand the moment
when the theatre must come down

When Lead Soldiers Ruled

If it is necessary
to observe the mechanical
and mathematical manifestations
of the human mind
spin out into exponential presentations
of hollow beings
so be it

If it is necessary
for the distortions
of refracted stardust
to blind the third eye
of Man
so be it

Know that the magnificence
of every expression
will and must rise
Life force cannot fail
for that which is eternal
must always return
to itself

From this place of Home
looking back upon the journey
Humankind will smile
recalling a childhood
when toys became alive
in our dreams
and the lead soldiers
threatened to rule the world

Leaders
teachers and scientists
put down your habits

DEAR HUMAN CHILD

and suppositions
Lay the familiar to rest
for without death
there is no way
to be born anew

MAY 2006

What is the meaning of
spiritual darkness?

The great teachers and philosophers of the ages have all had to face this question, yet never has the shadow been more important to understand than now, as darkness seems to rise upon our Earth with every passing day. That which we call Evil is a trickster, seeking to distract, divide, and instill fear in a purposeful way. It is so tempting to slip into the mindset of warfare; and yet, if we can understand that all polarities hold meaning, is it possible that the greatest duality of all may hold its own invitation to unity?

I have had my own dance with the dark, when someone very dear to me, a truly light-filled soul, was pulled into realms of suffering I had thought lived only in the fiction of Tolkien. Thus this topic holds great personal meaning for me, and is the theme of the second book in this series of collected transmissions. It is my belief that until now we have dared to speak only to the tip of the iceberg, while many fathoms below move massive forces, not separate from us, but rather the mirrored impulses of our own separation from truth.

In this transmission, we begin with a new way of seeing our dualistic world in the archetype of breath that threads throughout our experience of life. Read aloud and discuss this transmission with a friend to explore guidance so fundamental to our changing world.

Cycles of Breath

To walk upon the Earth
is to be a child
and to be a child is to live
without full knowledge
in a state of innocence
learning
and grace
And what child
does not love to hear a story
full of adventure
of quests
of fearful events
challenges overcome
and then finally
a rightful peace returned
that has been
well earned

So when you ask
as a child

Cycles of Breath

there is mystery here
that cannot be grasped
by the child's mind
and yet
all will one day become clear
in her readiness
to grow up
to step fully
into the world of dreams
and the world
of fears

For while we say
that only Love is real
there are many faces
to the love you may know
in a life
and our guidance comes
to lead you toward
the recognition of this Love
in every moment
and beneath every shadow
that may appear

Be aware
for example
that the terms
of our descriptions
are given intentionally
as concepts
that are familiar to you
so you may learn
by the example
of the structures
of your world

DEAR HUMAN CHILD

But know also
that a much greater perspective exists
that may not be witnessed
from where you stand
and so language
becomes weak
and only the knowing of the heart
may finally
take you there

The rhythm
of the heart
and of the breath
is at the essential core
of the universe
in its nature
Breath is life
and life is active
It expands
and it contracts
in a fluidity
that is the hallmark
of its existence

There is no life
without breath
as there is no breath
without expansion
and retreat
The universe breathes
It has always breathed
and always will
in one form of inhalation
or exhalation

Cycles of Breath

at all times
In this we find
the presence of polarity
and therefore the gift
of opposition
and flow

It has been said
that god has chosen
to see his reflection
in human kind
to observe divinity
through the objectivity
of distance
and therefore separation

Consider
that the essence of Spirit
of God/Goddess
under so many names
may in fact
have embodied polarity
throughout time
for the cycles of breath
of life
to be
in their inherently creative form

The vastness of this
cannot be grasped
by the linear mind
by the usual seeking
but only through the experience
of the body that breathes

that inhales its first breath
and continues to expand
and contract
until its final breath
in the physical form
And so
when we
as living beings
entered the home
of our universe
we did so
not as playthings
of any higher power
but as
expressions
of the force that defines
All That Is
as essential
to the divine
as the first cries
of an infant
upon the exhale
of a Universe
that will breathe forever
upon the elimination
of Time

When a child breathes
does she regret
what leaves her lungs
to make way
for what she will take in?
Or does she trust
that the symbiosis
of this process

Cycles of Breath

is the source
of all joy
of all purity
and the answer
to her prayers
for peace?

Is not
this acknowledgement
of rotational polarity
as the essence of Spirit
the meaning of Oneness
as it has been described
not
as a state
where otherness has been eliminated
but where
the cycles of duality
of separateness
are observed to link
into the circular
which is the infinite
which is the most blessed shape
that lives within
every facet
of this
and every
world?

And too
within this perception
of existence
must be found rhythm
must be found

the beating of the heart
and the hand
upon a drum
the day
and the night
the turning
of the seasons
the course
of the tides
the birthing
and the dying
the love
and the fear
the laughter
and the wailing
each one
upon a breath
as it leaves
and it comes

And so
if there is to be
the brilliance
of divine light
there also must be
the greatest dark
that has run
as far as it can travel
away from Love
and this
has been named as Evil
in its essential distance
from the source
of its birth

Cycles of Breath

Evil
has so many faces
in your world
so many names
and manifestations
and yet
it is but one expression
and that is the hopelessness
that comes
when light seems unreachable
and so darkness is embraced
as the only power
to be seen

Evil
is the breath of God
upon the furthest exhale
the furthest distance
the final note
of the last song
before the readiness has come
for a new note
the next breath
that will return us
within the cycle
of Love

As such
it is nothing distinct
nothing separate from
the All
and yet
at such a distance
there are few creatures

with sufficient faith
to remember
to see the light
through the blindness
that Evil entails

In this way
there seems great power here
when darkness seems to enter
and to remain
and yet
we must remind you
that each soul
knows
and holds
its own relationship
with Evil
and as such
there is no power present
beyond the strength
of each individual
in the recognition
of their own fear

And know also
that when the breath is expelled
an inhalation of Spirit must come
for there is no end
to the circle
there is no separation
between God the light
and God the dark
and this process will be
as it has always been

Cycles of Breath

long past
any dalliances of our confusion
any wars
any destruction
any
of the many blindnesses
in the travels
of humankind

It is this structure
of variance
that gives life
and gives permission
for power
and light
to be accepted
and received
This is not
a reason for suffering
but rather
an explanation
of how stagnation
is not peace
of how the death
you fear
is a *final* death
an ending
that cannot be
cannot exist
within the cycles
of Love

This is why
all

that you so often see
as Evil
must be expressed
as faithlessness
as a need to control
what is ultimately feared
for the blindness then
has come
and the understanding
of a return to the light
has been lost
in one moment
of one life

Yet know this
that there is no way
to remove the breath of life
from that
which is infinite
and immortal
therefore
the role of darkness
is critical
as it offers a counterpoint
to illuminate
the light
that never dies
and in this way
it is not suffering
but our leaving of suffering
that awakens us
that brings us to the door
of growing beyond
the human child

Cycles of Breath

It is
polarity
that grants us choice
and choice
that gives us the freedom
to become
what we already are
for movement
is our truth
our nature
and our brilliance
with no ending
ever
ever
in sight

And so
there is no peace
that was left behind
in order to taste
the hardships
of the earthly plane
No
instead there is peace
embedded in every moment
awaiting our discovery
as we step back
and back
from the limitations of our fear
until the wholeness
the Oneness
of experience
is found

DEAR HUMAN CHILD

That which we name
as danger
is the locus
of collective fear
and it will become
according to our rhythms
our expressions
as we are afraid
Yet
the truth of existence
is Love
and truth
is never lost
only hidden
for a time

When we choose
know that choice is powerful
as an expression
of whatever aspect of God
we may allow
in that particular breath
but also know
that even
the most horrific darkness found
in the imaginations of men
will be brought into balance
must be brought into balance
beyond the boundaries
of our perceptions
of space and time

And so
children play

Cycles of Breath

as through your games
great truth is found
and the more Truth
you remember
the more peace
may be experienced
as you ride
the breath of all
that is All
that is Divine

As this exhalation
prepares to end
we feel the urgency
of a new breath
ready to begin
Yet trust
that there is nothing to die
and nowhere to end
in the Love that lives forever
beyond all our visions
greater than any universe
larger than anything
we can dream

JANUARY 2019

What does it mean to have
soul freedom in apocalyptic
times?

We long for principles to help us through the dark when it comes, simplicity and clarity to lead us. It is one thing to understand and another to implement. This transmission lays out fundamentals to guide our hearts even on difficult days. Consider writing out the teaching points in your journal to help them land more deeply in your awareness.

So many teachings warn us that we now live in what the Vedas describe as the Kali Yuga, an age of materialism and dissolution into chaos, darkness and suffering, or what the Hopi call the Fourth World. The last of four cycling yugas, it may help us to remember that every age must come to an end to make way for the next. This is the principle of expansion and contraction, and while we live in a time of darkness which seems to increase daily, if we can surrender to trusting even this experience, we are poised to play our part in the accompanying shift. Every time we choose to return to our own expansive state, we contribute to the resolution of the Kali Yuga.

Our inner work calls us to be present with the shadow, and yet not drown in it. To never deny and yet to always alchemically transform. This transmission offers seven clearly described principles to root us in stability, even when faced with challenge and fear. Notice if one confronts you, or leaps off the page with truth; read it aloud and journal your responses. These are life-changing principles, when we dare to allow.

The Light That Is

We begin with an understanding
of what it means to choose

Without the power of choice there is no freedom
Without freedom there is no capacity for choice
Without the threat of anarchy
there is no awareness of Divine order
Without godliness found in every moment
there is no meaning discovered in human form
Without the hard work of earning awareness
nothing will be treasured
Without the rebellious child
there is no separation from the Mother/Father God
Without an unconditionally loving Parent
there is no coming Home

Do you see
how we must first be *here*
in order to go *there*?
Do you recognize

The Light That Is

there must be silence
for music to be born?
Can you allow
that in order to remember an exquisite truth
it must be forgotten for a time?

We do not speak of choice
to encourage you to play with power
We do not call you to ownership
for you to steal what you think you need
because you falsely believe in lack

We instead offer you an opportunity to witness
to understand
instead of hiding beneath the blankets
in your self-made night
to avoid the dark you think is outside

There is a magnificence to all creation
invisible only to those
who live disconnected
from an acceptance of Divine Love

These are the days of returning
to all that once gave meaning to our world

One:
**Learn the practice of choosing Love
and see how it eases your pain**

In every experience of challenge or loss
we are given the chance to choose from our fear
or liberate the voice of holy Love from within us
We can become distracted and delayed by vengeance
or we can Love

DEAR HUMAN CHILD

We can hate the people
the circumstances of our pain
or we can Love
We can believe in failure
in a disordered Universe
or we can feel Love as a force
larger than any physical experience
larger than thought
larger even than shame

We can look upon our crumbling house
and wish it to be different
or we can look upon it with a heart wide open
and let it fall to the dust of Mother Earth
where we may begin again

This force is not romantic
it is not personal
it is beyond human
it lives in our willingness to choose it
until no matter what the question
it gives us answers over and over again

When confronting every attacker
this field of immortal radiance is always stronger
than the weapons of our fear
not by meeting blood with blood
but by transporting the physical
through a portal
where no one can lose
and there is nothing to be gained

You have heard stories of ascension
of transcendence
of miracles

The Light That Is

These are not stories
but rather Love at work
and the very particles of the material
become digested
as if under the beam of a laser
and Love is revealed
as all that remains

What does this look like
for the ordinary woman or man?
Expect that you have access to the miraculous
and you will
Ask for the impossible
and it will arrive
Join your voices together in announcing
what was once unthinkable
and you will create it
before your very eyes

Two:
When experiencing fear or rage
do not give it away
but make it your own

We who walk upon the back of this planet
live within one thin layer
of identifiable experience
These elements are shifting and melding
and we begin to see
what was once denied

Energy forms of all kinds
intersect with our human lives
Like breath on a cold day
we exhale aspects of our fears

and they take shape in the very air before us
They are hungry for another breath
and another
and so long as we feed them
they will cloud our eyes

Just as cancer is a biological element
which feeds mistakenly upon its own life
and then kills its host
the demonic needs our fear and helplessness
to take shape
Without our cooperation
these forces themselves
diminish and die

How do I live beyond fear? you ask
You look it in the eye
Stand quaking
in the God Love of your own heart
and dare anything else
to deny you this
for it cannot

The greatest beasts of our nightmares
may be purified
by our choice to deny them
the food of our fear
Cast blind faith of Love upon them instead
and they will melt before our eyes

Three:
Come together

When we slipped from our mother's womb
we fell into the idea of separateness

The Light That Is

When we meet an enemy upon the path
we are vulnerable to them
because we think them to be
something other than ourselves

But when we consciously choose to stand in the presence
of one another instead
and tell the truth of Love
the power of its radiance exponentially becomes manifold
Where there was once two together
four are born
Where once four gazed eye to eye
sixteen begin to sing
Where sixteen vibrate in this presence
hundreds of thousands are lifted up
Where nations fall upon their knees in union
all humanity and fellow species turn around
to join in a unity of essence
global healing
and inherent rebirth
Come together
in whatever form of Love
speaks through you
and you will change the world

Four:
Tell the truth without blame

For centuries humankind has lived in a dark alley
between fakery and judgement
either pretending to be something
in order to seek safety
or amputating aspects of ourselves
through blame, vengeance and retribution

as if this would somehow
ease the pain

Dare instead to stand before yourselves
and others
in the absolute whole
of your nature
Do not attempt to be anything other than what you are
and do not regret any part of what you see
in your own mirror
In profound self-acceptance
lives all forgiveness of others
and in the release of accusation
arrives the Divine Mystery of resolution

Take this one step
and discover how the talons
of the next creature who wishes to prey upon you
have nowhere to take hold
You become instead the liquid light
of your own essence
impossible to damage
lose or deny

Five:
Believe in what you cannot see
and allow yourself to see
what you believe in your heart to be true

Let go of the literal
for there is no answer to be found here
In fact
most of what gives your material world meaning
exists beyond the sight of your physical eyes
But there is another kind of sight which awaits you

and once awakened
it will never again sleep
This knowing begins in the aspect of your being
born out of a marriage between Heart and Spirit
It cannot be described but only lived
and once lived
it never dies

This is the God Self
the presence of the expanded nature
and this Self is unaffected by the dance of
visual illusion
and instead is fully guided
by a multi-dimensional fluidity
This Self knows no time
and no limitation
because fear of how things *seem* to look
has transmuted into Creation
an expression
according to each moment
of being

Yes this is magic
and it is happening everywhere
if you are ready to see it
feel it
allow it to be

This is the reward of the end of thinking
and the allowing of expanded sensation
This is like the transition from drawing
stick figures in black and white
to the dreams of an altered consciousness
kaleidoscopic

inter-dimensional
and responsive to your every playful wish

Why would you choose to live in one dimension
when all existence lives in infinite expression?

It is not as far as you think
nor as strange as you fear
but rather it is an act of surrender
like the feverish child who
finally settles into the lullaby
of his mother's arms

Six:
Stop waiting

Our dalliances with protection
weigh us down
like a swimmer wearing armour
of steel
There is no more time to wait
because there is no more Time
And once you begin to really see
this you will feel
What was once tomorrow becomes yesterday
this we know
but it is also true
that what was once a hundred years in the future
can become Now in the blink of an eye
bringing with it
a century of history
and more

Without Time
there is no need to wait

but instead we are greeted
by the invitation to immerse ourselves
in immediate Creation
instantaneous activation
with absolute ease

It is important to note
that this capacity for choosing Now
can only take place
in that state of Grace
for this is the nature of timelessness
It knows no boundaries
no either/or
no risk
and no rules

It is matter becoming the liquid
of our souls' desires

Seven:
**Make art so that you may discover
you are Art**

Whatever form of expression calls you
it is the juices of your arousal
the notes of your perfect choir
the tears of your ecstasy
In truth there is nothing but Creation
and our pain has lived
in the confusion that art is an extra
for a chosen
or a broken few

When you chose incarnation
to be a part of this revolution of Being

you began to make art
When you spoke your first words
you wrote poetry
When you took your first steps
you danced
When you touched your first petal
you created a sculpture
When you first wept
you formed symphonies
of spiralling truths

There is nothing but Art
and it needs no wall
to hang upon
There is nothing but expression
and communication
because all Beingness is flow
which must be given and received

There is nothing wrong in your art
because there is nothing outside of it
and once in it
you give yourself the greatest gift
you will ever know
the perception of Self
for which Source hungered
when the beings of this realm
were born
When the Divine said
Let there be Light
what was truly spoken was
Let the Light that is
be seen

The Light That Is

There is nothing else
and so the darkness of these times
bows down before us
the Truth revealed

With this blessing
your sufferings are more beautiful
in our eyes
than any mountain of gems
In this
you have chosen
well

guardian

OCTOBER 2023

The night is dark, but the
dawn will come.

As the world watches, the horror of vengeance, war, and oppression play out in the Middle East. Thousands of children are dying. No end is in sight. So many who feel helpless are asking, "How do we understand this conflict? How do we respond to such overwhelming suffering?"

This transmission may push the reader past comfort zones into a deeper level of witness to the great tragedies of humanity. It is so tempting to take sides, to make ancient hate and familiar feuds an excuse to respond in kind. Yet where does this take us, except back around the karmic wheel once more?

When we dare to choose a wider, higher view, we begin to see the deep teachings being offered to the collective. It may break our hearts to think that so many innocents suffer to learn these lessons; but from a karmic perspective, we have all played all roles. We have all stood as saviour, we have all acted as the persecutor, and we have all lived lives as helpless victims of unconscious war. This is the learning of our dense, earthly realm. We were born to experience the expansion of consciousness, and Creation lives to experience us.

The very experience of reading this transmission is an act of peace. Read it again. Read it aloud. Use your voice to lift yourself up, and we all rise with you.

Demon of Division

Cruelty
begets cruelty
which teaches us
that we are all Divine
and we are all capable
of the demonic

Only when we are
finally able
to understand this
may we exorcise the power
of the dark

It is not just
that we are meant
to no longer take sides
to no longer say
I stand with this one
I stand with that one
but when we agree

Demon of Division

to see the inherent shadow
within us all
we tell the truth
and when we tell the truth
we are humbled
and when we are humbled
we return to peace

There is no one to fight
and no one
to fear
There is only One

Conquerors
sewers of vengeance
when you reach toward God
know that
the devil reaches
with you

When you suggest
that God is on your side
whenever you use God's name
to justify harm in this way
be it Yahweh
Allah or Christ
the devil speaks through you
and this is
the inherent risk
of any attempt
to organize God

For the heart of Man
is most weak

when he presumes to suggest
that his own fear
his own broken need
knows anything
of the Divine
The idea of God
uttered in human fear
is the furthest thing
from holy

There is
no holy war
There is
no holy hate
And there is never
ever
such a thing
as holy vengeance
for there is no god
of any name
who celebrates this
base human emotion
To suggest otherwise
reveals only
how far we are willing
to travel
from the truth of
Divine Love
to justify our own
unholy games

The sacred
is now fully absent
from these lands

Demon of Division

where once
the prophets roamed
There is nothing righteous here

In the willingness
to harm one child
just one
all grace is gone
no matter what
is written
no matter what
is believed

A weapon which
touches a child
is held
in the devil's hand
for religion
is the attempt of Man
to organize
his own dreams
of power
through the lens
of his own fear
and unconscious hunger

While there is
divinity in every moment
religious warfare
is nothing but
the negative image of the Divine
that which we call evil
on all sides
and in all forms

DEAR HUMAN CHILD

True faith
does not divide
it embraces
True consciousness
never blames
but only heals
True love
owns nothing
not land
and not people

True wisdom
seeks no power
but rather transforms
suffering through faith
consciousness
and love
Love takes no sides
for it is whole
Holy
Whole

Love is a pulsing sphere
and hate is but a circle
yet each will come back
unto itself
So where is God
you ask
when children die
when safety is stolen?
And the answer
is always, always
that Love is the choice
we make

Demon of Division

in every moment
between the shadow
and light
within our own hearts

It is the day
when each soul rises
that the world
will transform

The day when
nation
race and religion
dissolve into One
But until we are ready
the demon of division
will rise
will grow
will feed upon our fear
our spite
turning the sky black
with our own thoughts
and the rivers red
with the blood of those who die
in innocence and ignorance
until the choice
of their souls
to return and live once more
is made
in the realm of the opportunity
of another human day

Know this

DEAR HUMAN CHILD

your flags
mean nothing
your borders
mean nothing
your military forces
your displays
of righteous retaliation
mean nothing
when seen through the eyes
of Creator

So lift yourselves up
you children
of the history of hate
rise higher
than who you think you are
Notice how easily
the very fires
which burned your ancestors
now fall
from your own lips
over and over
until you are ready to see
you slaughter
your own cousins
your own sisters and brothers
you rape your own mothers
and torture your own fathers
You make hell
for your own children
until you choose
until you *choose*
to be the authors
of your own fate

Demon of Division

And yes
the lies are everywhere
And yes
the powerful
hold the greatest
capacity for evil
because they dance
with the greatest
capacity for good
They have forgotten
alchemy
The demon of division
has seduced their souls
They have become
the masters of illusion
who claim to be
protectors of the lambs
while quietly inviting
the lion
to eat his fill

Nothing is as it seems
because the old illusions
must fall
and the more tightly
we hold
to how we think it should be
the more painful
the rebirth will seem
in the grip
of our comfortable
fears

The truth is

DEAR HUMAN CHILD

Love is easy
so much easier
than you might think
While vengeance is hard
and eats up everything good
within the soul
Forgiveness
has nothing to do
with the blame
to which you cling
And brutality
is never new
for it breeds and grows
in the gardens
the prisons
and the ghettos
we create

But once revenge is spawned
it will initiate armies of peace
a great rising
of the many millions of aspects
of Divine Consciousness
to come together
resistance
of the highest order
as the devil
dissolves
starved to death
by our refusal
to feed
what is not born
of true Grace

Demon of Division

Be not afraid
for there is no power greater
than our willingness
to love
beyond borders
beyond religion
beyond our forefathers'
ancient hate

The day must come
when we do unto others
not what has been done to us
but rather what
pure Love
commands

We are asked to understand
that no conflict
no suffering is one-sided
There is always a mutuality
a collaboration for
the victim/persecutor dance
lives within us all
The persecutor
can only exist in relation
to the victim
and so
when we lift a victim up
into the development
of their own power
persecution loses its hold

If we can turn our gaze away
for a moment

from the proud
the fierce
the righteous persecutor
and look instead
toward lifting up those
who have found themselves
in the land of the victim
division has the opportunity
to transform
and the new consciousness
arise
This is the perfect
invitation
of our times
To lift up
means to shed the identity
of victim
It generates a strength
which has nothing to do
with attack or counter attack
This strength runs deeper
than any primitive
child-like rage
for only he who holds
a broken child within
is capable of cruelty
to other children
in turn

Until awareness rises
the circle of hate
must always return

As the world bears witness

Demon of Division

to Nakba once more
we may ask
how many times
must suffering come
how many lives
how many losses
how much horror
before we learn?

It is the gift of those who suffer
to awaken those
who have been afraid to see
and from the stage
of this act
of human theatre
it may seem so difficult to understand
how even in this horror
there is no mistake
under Heaven

We are asked to consider
that it is the darkness
which allows the light
to illuminate
and if we look to
every great leader
teacher
or wisdom keeper
throughout human history
these souls
have known suffering
the very suffering
which created their strength
To wish

DEAR HUMAN CHILD

an easy life
upon a soul
is to take from them
the source
of their gifts

Instead
we witness the final throes
of the shadow upon our Earth
flushed into awareness
like a flock of birds
from a bush
and we allow our hearts
to open wide
to every grieving family
every terrified child
and say
You cannot know
just how much love
is all around you
How many souls
are beside you
How deeply your pain
is felt and understood
Even when it seems
all have abandoned you
You are not alone
you are not alone
you are not alone

But we also say
to those who are able-bodied
who may live a world away
from these scenes of horror

Demon of Division

Stand up and speak
Stand up and care
Put aside your fear
of opposing or being opposed
You are as much a part
of the unfolding
as those who inhabit
the physical experience
of this oppression
and this war
If you do not know how
simply ask
your own aching heart
and you will find
your path

When purpose and meaning
are discovered
our pain is eased
So please
do not give this honour away
to your gods
You are the owner
you are the shapeshifter
you are the one
who creates poetry
out of hurt
and soon you will begin
to witness
how there is magic in the heartbreak
for there is no angel
who regrets their days
of living and dying
in the human way

DEAR HUMAN CHILD

The night is dark
but the dawn will come
The remembering
of affection and compassion
will one day surpass
the need to divide
and own
and destroy

Your daily thoughts
your moment to moment
willingness
to envision and act
in the glory of an utterly new world
has so much more power
than you know

You
and you
and the many
are the answer
to every question
you hold

MAY 2020

Did you know your words are
a holy force?

In my cellular healing work, I receive detailed, personal, past-life stories to assist the soul in releasing karmic trauma. It is so that Time in its truth exists beyond the linear; yet as we read these words, we live upon this Earth in an agreement to have a human experience, and thus to live in a world defined by human senses.

So much of our present is driven by unconscious memory of the other selves we have lived. I have received numerous initiatory readings from gifted intuitives, revealing lifetimes of terrible suffering. In one reading, I was told of a life in which my vocal cords were cut out as a sacrifice. This kind of story is not uncommon with sensitive and old souls, and thus so many carry wounds related to expression. Often as we begin to heal, the quiet one speaks too loudly, while the loud one pauses in silence. We discover that what we say is more than information. Our words are ripe with the power to create.

Imagine, then, the power of the collective, simmering with awakening to communications of all kinds. Imagine the arguments, the surprises. Imagine the truths, imagine the lies. This is our world. This is the language of our times.

How do you use your voice? What are you waiting to say? What can you speak into being, in the revelation of your expressive gifts?

The Force of Words

Words are the symbols of our voices
They represent
but even more
they carry
as they move

Whether we speak them with our eyes
or our lips
whether we hear them with our ears
or our hearts
they move
and they move within us
They are the tools
of the soul's desires

Silence is the birthplace
of words
Silence was present
before words were known
and will be there

The Force of Words

when they die
This time is coming
there will be an end to the age
of the necessity of spoken language
but until this dawning
words represent
everything we have

Communication is only necessary
where separation exists
We only reach to understand
what we fear we do not
We only speak what we believe
needs to be heard
We only answer
when we want it to be known
that we have heard
and we wish to be heard
in return

There are places where silence is king
where the imposition of communication
is seen as a distraction
from the power of inner peace
The keepers of temples and monasteries
know this
as do
those who walk in meditation halls
and sleeping hospitals
or anywhere an infant rests
a prayer is dreamt
or a choir prepares to sing

The value of Silence is found
in the awareness of what is not spoken

which thus makes way
for true Presence to appear
Yet
when we come together
two by two
and more
we are immediately drawn to find our words
to express
and through expression connect
and through connection
remember who we are
For the Creator said
Let there be Light
and in this speaking
the possibility of Light
was born

We have been invited
to consider before we express
is it necessary?
is it true?
is it kind?
to pause
to count to ten
to breathe
to sleep for a night
before we send the letter
to give space for discernment
in regard to what we dare to say

Yet so often
in these times of magnification
language has become a weapon
a tool itself of destruction

The Force of Words

of falsehood
of false pride
Even between those who love
expression spills out
in rages and torrents
the language of hatred and vilification
of judgement and separation
uttering the constant reminder
that you and I are not the same
that you embody a problem I perceive
that in your differences from me
I am threatened
or you are lost
or the whole world will collapse
beneath the weight of your lies

The compulsion to speak
the contradiction to your beliefs
has become so great in me
your ignorance such an irritant
your mistakes so dangerous
that to tear you down
becomes my momentary pleasure
to put to right
your right to be wrong

What is so interesting
is that we observe this in the conversation
of adults
of those who walk in grown bodies
and yet if our children dare to contradict
to disrespect
they are quickly silenced
for insurrection cannot be tolerated
when control is at stake

DEAR HUMAN CHILD

So is this not
what we witness here
in a world where information
populates and spreads like a virus
ever mutating
always feeding upon its latest host
and thus becoming formed
by the blood
the breath of the one who speaks it
the child *within* the adult
the one who was once so shushed
in turn
the one who fears
the one who aches
the one who is desperate
to regain that lost control?

To choose Silence
is to invite a state of Grace
To be forced into silence
is to be denied the connection
which leads to Love
and these are the days
these are the times
wherein all our untended wounds
must cleanse
wherein every fear
must be revealed

So wherever the touch of love
has been denied within our own soul's journey
our voices now rise up
Wherever we perceive
we have been told no

The Force of Words

we now must say yes
Wherever we have been kept
from knowing a truth
we now will find new lies
And whatever world we fear the most
we will create
as whatever we are so afraid to lose
will seem to fly out our window
As this vision rises
before our expectant eyes
we will utter the words:
Hear me
for my truth is the only truth
and if you see something different
you are wrong

So picture this:
The deepest wounds
of every soul
incarnate upon this Earth
seek healing in their expression
at the same time
The voices of every creator
form words of activation
simultaneously
making concrete
that which must be seen
to be released

The conversations
of each being
seek to generate the matrix
of their own beliefs
because they must

and so the world becomes
many worlds
many visions
so many fears
all intersecting
all reaching for validation
all seeing
what they choose to see
which is indeed how it must be
for each one of us to begin to discover
the power and the magic
which lives within us
splinters of the Divine Creator
all

When we open our machines
our ears
our eyes each day
we are shown an expanse of illusions
like pages ripped out of a book of fairytales
and blowing everywhere across the land
tumbling over top of one another
spreading upon the wind
rich with fables of good and evil
saviours and demons
the darkest of suffering
and the most magical discoveries
of jewels and feasts
and even love
and it is all true
and it is all a lie
as we choose
to make it so

The Force of Words

What is the way forward
for those who wish
to lead with heart?
Simply this:
Let go of the idea of immutable fact
and embrace allowing the truth
of what you *feel*
When you are confronted
in conversation
interpret what you are shown
through your heart
for this is the way you will discover meaning
and meaning
is the only timeless version
of Truth
there is

Acknowledge that when you converse
you are initiating
an exchange of energy
represented by your letters and words
a flow of liquid intent
both conscious and unconscious
and this is exactly
how it is meant to be
This is the ultimate purpose
of our utterances
and their reason for being

Decide what form of energy
you would like to embody
and let your words originate
from this essence
Consider what form of blessing

you would like to receive
from the expressions of others
Take what you need
and leave the rest
for what is a match for you
will always
be offered
everywhere you turn

Dare to allow yourself to shape the world
by becoming one who listens
when all are shouting
and one who speaks
what is rarely heard

And above all
trust this moment
with all of its chaotic voices
This cleansing was foretold
in the beginning
and must be lived
till its end
The inner children of our species
must be adolescents for a time
before they are ready to walk
as adults
to speak the language of a mature Love
Pity no one
for each soul has a role to play
and every voice you hear
was once yours too

There is only one thing
more contradictory to soul freedom

The Force of Words

than imposed silence
and that is
imposed belief
and so the present moment permission
to resist perceived shackles
is a gift
a rebellion that had to come
and so long as this wave is followed
by a second wave
of more heightened awareness
we will soon embark upon a time
when enemies become collaborators
and every kind of voice
joins the same choir
sour notes sung
until they can be sung no more
and only harmony echoes
across seas and mountains
a long-lost song
remembered
from our birth

Your words
are more than words
they are a holy force
ready to move
the frozen hearts
of the gods of every land
Let that force be born of Love
and Beauty
and may you listen
and receive
as never before

DECEMBER 2016

What do you resist, and how
do you surrender?

This is a personal transmission received for a woman who wanted to understand her own internal fear.

It can be helpful to recognize that resistance is a simple word to describe the polarities of attachment and aversion that live within us all. An important way to begin the dismantling of resistance is to release any self-shame or blame we hold about our reactivity, so we are better positioned to transform it.

Whether we respond with habitual passivity or rage, healing lies in our willingness to witness that which lives beneath and observe the teaching offered in every moment.

Resistance is the fuel which generates the potential for realignment. The hand that pulls back the bow, creating deep tension, is the means by which the arrow will reach its target. If we aim our arrow to fly far, we can expect that a tension equal to that distance will present itself in our lives. This is no error. This is an energetic law in action.

The teaching that our greatest sorrow holds the potential to serve our greatest liberation is found in many spiritual traditions. When we feel lost in the midst of our pain or struggle, we may not be able to touch this awareness, but we can always practice surrender to Trust.

Dear reader, you may notice that the word trust is very present in so many transmissions and commonly with an uppercase T. This capitalization invites us to see Trust differently. So often we feel that to trust someone means we assume they will not hurt or betray us; yet this is expectation, not trust. The deeper meaning of Trust is that we understand the purposeful nature of all experience, even that which may be painful, that which we may not yet have integrated into our awareness. We recognize we are all players upon a vast stage of human theatre and beyond the characters we inhabit lives a united consciousness and a Divine unfolding that grants meaning to all.

As you read this guidance, feel into your own heart to better understand the source of your own resistance. Where does it live in the physical body? How does it express in the emotional body? Where is the root of your liberation which awaits to be found?

Become Instead the Willow

All growth
all process of depth
requires one element
that is universal in its nature
that crosses the boundaries
of culture
religion
and time
and this is Trust
the state
that may only be achieved
through the surrender
of our fear
into the hands of our own
experience
of the divine

DEAR HUMAN CHILD

Trust is
the state of grace
that allows us to fall into
the natural rhythms
of our being
the state
that lets us
let go
of our fear that we are travelling
too fast
and yet moving
too slow

Trust is the acceptance
that lets us live in present joy
instead of future longing
or past fear
and it is born
out of complete knowing
that whatever comes to us
it is the right thing
even if it arrives
wrapped in pain
even if
we do not yet understand
how
or why

In this search
for the crossroads of the soul
that place
where your willingness
runs up against a sign
that will not be bypassed

Become Instead the Willow

cannot be
overlooked
we guide you to an awareness
that you are thirsty here
for the taste of Trust
and its absence
dictates so much
of your experience
in this world

The child in you
has not believed in safety
for a very long time
She believes herself to be
as vulnerable upon the Earth
as a living but captured insect
pinned through the heart
displayed upon a mounting board
for examination
under the scrutiny of her peers
and her God
unable to escape
unable to even move
but for the struggle
the endless struggle
to stay alive

Her spirit
is that of the warrior
and so she does fight
she fights hard and long
against the injustice
that seems everywhere
She resists

the entrapment that she
experiences
with all her will
and the sensation
of immobility
causes her to react
with a dramatic response
the flailing
of a death throe
while others watch calmly
whispering
Why does she struggle so?
Why does she not simply accept
and give in?

All the while
in her heart
is deep betrayal
deep grief
that no one else
seems to bear witness
to her pain
and so she offers this too
to the world
crying out
Can you not see me
where is your compassion
am I nothing to you
and you
and you
as I suffer
in this way?

But the news

Become Instead the Willow

the truth
we bring to you today
is the offer of awakening
to the awareness
that your perception
of this struggle
is your own
that this resistance
is in fact
your own
and that the experience
of distance
from your loved ones
of a cool observation
of your suffering
This too
is created
by your patterns of belief
and thus
is the comparable moment
of transformation
also your own
to hold

Please begin
with a focus upon understanding
the deeper origins
of your pain
You are aware
on a daily basis
of the emotion
in your body
but this awareness runs
only at the level of expression

DEAR HUMAN CHILD

as the frightened animal
who panics within the net
of her capture
does not see
that her struggle
actually embeds her capture
and that the road to her freedom
lies in surrender
and a calm
that will guide her
and carry her
home

In order to begin
to cultivate this calm
you must first
explore the nature
of the pain that has brought you
to this place of fear
through a depth of examination
that speaks only
to your soul
your heart
your fear
and the wounding
that lies within

The child of yours
fears great loss
for she has known great loss
and this must be expressed
in a slow
soft
deep, deep surrender to the pain

Become Instead the Willow

that will take time
courage
and support
from the very loved ones
you have been afraid
to lose

Next
will come the consciousness
that may emerge from your pain
of the practice
of coming to know your strength
in a new way
the strength
not of reactivity
but of Trust
of knowing
that you cannot die
you will not die
that you are
the immortality of God's love
and that all danger
is the illusion
of our mistaken belief
in loss

This empowerment
may at first
look and feel
like powerlessness
because you are asked
to give up the struggle
and instead
sink into an acceptance

that must live
at a deep level
of knowing
in body, heart, and mind

Instead of the fear
and the quick vulnerability
turn instead
to the god
that is present in you
in every moment
the acceptance
of the path that your own soul
has chosen
in this world

You have been
the burning bush
alive with fire
of immolation
Become instead
the willow
her feet firmly planted
in deep wet soil
as she bends with the wind
and dips to touch
the nearby waters
that flow and flow
with a gracious understanding
that the rain
does not die
but merely enters the streams
and the streams
do not die

Become Instead the Willow

but merely enter the river
and the rivers
do not die
but merely enter the oceans
and the oceans
do not die
but merely feed the clouds
who weep the rains
that feed the willow herself
as all Life
that travels the cycle
of loss and rebirth
which is
the very gift of awareness
we have chosen
in this world

We guide you
to walk each day
with a surrender not only
to your pain
but to your joy
for there is nothing
to control
nothing to judge
and nothing
to protect yourself from
once you escape
from your own memories
your own constructs
of entrapment and fear

Your power is barely begun
for it will be found

in the passion of peace
in the maturity of grace
and the opening
of a heart
that is rich with untapped love
awaiting her moment of freedom
from these ancient fears

Watch your own growth
as you have felt watched
by others
Forgive yourself
as you have wished
to be forgiven by others
Above all
Trust
that every experience
is of your own making
and that Spirit is with you
in every expression
and so there is no danger
no action
and no escape necessary
for you lie
at all times
in the arms
of your god

JULY 2020

Some spiritual paths guide us to look
only to the light, others guide us to
look the shadow in the eye. Where
should our attention lie?

We all hold protections and defences against feeling emotional pain. I think of this as the simplest definition of what we commonly call ego: the habitual avoidance of directly addressing and releasing our fear. We could even name this as a central characteristic of the human condition and, with the rise of the popularity of the Law of Attraction, permission to avoid the shadow was proposed.

"Look only at what feels good," they said. Keep your focus only upon the positive, and give no space for oppositional energy in your life. Train your mind what to believe, and this will make manifest all your desires. It is a tempting invitation, especially when accompanied by images of beautiful, young people living in wealth and pleasure. Absolutely, there is great power found in clarifying our vision while curbing our tendency to doubt and self-judge. However…

There is a fine line between calculated positivity and denial; and when we recognize that frequency never lies, we discover that no matter how much we may practise an affirmation, if the cellular memory of the body contradicts the message, it will not be heard. We are so much more than mind; we are perception and awareness that exist in the trans-personal realm. If we can accept that there is purpose in our suffering, the pain itself must be allowed to speak in order to reveal it. There is no bypassing this step. There is no cheat-sheet, no free pass, no exceptions. The alchemical transformation of our suffering is why we have incarnated in this dualistic realm; and in order to set ourselves free from our discomforts, we must first be willing to witness them. Awareness becomes consciousness, and that which is made conscious is set free.

Having dared to confront what is least pretty in our eyes, we are profoundly strengthened. Once we have taken the time to clear out the dusty basement of our house, then we are truly ready to paint and decorate. The emotional frequency of our earthly home will tell us what clutter we have hidden away and guide us toward the healing that awaits.

Imagine then, the power of cleansing the filthy basement of the entire collective. Imagine what it would look like to have corruption, cruelty, ignorance, and the unconscious elements of our institutions and systems all rise to the surface to be seen, so that together we may cleanse and prepare for the New Earth. If you can imagine this, you will better understand what we are witnessing globally in these days of the Shift. This is indeed the hallmark of our times.

Spiritual courage is the most beautiful of human qualities. May we discover such courage as individual souls and as One species in profound transition. When the lesson is learned, the teacher can go home.

Between Release and Ascension

This great question
lies at the heart
of the process of transmutation
It is one we all
so need to understand

You ask
do I turn my attention away from the wound
and feed only what lifts me up?
or do I allow the expression
of the hurt little one within
and respect her voice of pain?
The answer is yes to both
for one does not defy the other
in any way

When darkness comes
it can be as powerful

DEAR HUMAN CHILD

as a great wind
that blows out every candle
snuffs every flame
In the resulting absence of light
it seems that we are without choice
and made blind
to any avenue of relief

The truth is
there is always choice
and aspects of this permission
live in the mind
while other facets
live deep within the body
and express beyond the conscious voice

While the mind may indeed heal the body
in its powers of creation
we must be able to access thought
in order to take hold of such power
and to do this
we may first have to release
what is held in the physical form
overwhelming our senses
so that the mind may then find its way

This unfurling of energy can happen
without our awareness
but as we learn to pay attention
we discover ways
to drop deeply into an experience of our world
and learn to recognize this process
for what it is
until we know it

Between Release and Ascension

can feel it coming
just as a woman realizes when labour has begun
or a tumescent lover senses
the impending explosion
of sexual pleasure and release

Each soul in body
holds its own vibration
and its own level of awareness of this
To very many
these principles are so unconscious
it is like every day walking on silk and velvet
wearing heavy rubber boots

Others have been activated
and a detoxification has begun
the cleansing of many lives
and many wounds
experiencing stages of purification
that are as intense as the original wounding
triggering despair
and a crisis of faith
Then there are those
who have already walked these valleys of fire
discovering their own immortality
watching as pain becomes beautiful in its purity
and moments of saturated bliss are found
in a speck of floating dust

It is this place
where the practice of discernment
between release and ascension is found
and the irony is
that the deeper the surrender to the pain
the greater the thrust toward the light

DEAR HUMAN CHILD

At the same time
the more willing the detachment
from the story of the pain
the less its teeth will bite

The simplest direction
toward this sensual dance
is to view every sensation and emotion
without judgement
and with love
This perspective
will allow you to quickly sense
how to proceed
for it wipes away the tarnished clouds
of the self-critical seeker
who fears to love
what may seem unloving within

Any judgement of this kind
confuses the mind's ability
to facilitate release
If you Love your suffering when it rises
a broad, humble love without attachment
devoid of the victim's lament
the pain itself will speak to you
through your physical self
and above all your heart
giving you a direction to take
For the heart is the great mediator
between mind and body
the place where all truth lives
and may be experienced
as the kokoro of life

Between Release and Ascension

When the heart is open
if the pain is meant to intensify
and flow free
like the rush of a river through
a broken dam
then it will do so
and you will witness this
as grace

But if the expression of the wound
is simply a memory
an empty shadow that flickers
out of habit
then it will fall away easily
as you lift yourself up
into the Now
knowing this old wound
will never happen again

These answers may be found
both in the silence of divine listening
such as meditation
and also in the steps you walk each day
for the body holds its own wisdom
and will act
will sing its own song
even if the heart is not heard

So if you stumble
if you fall deep
Love even this moment
for every impulse of self-love
shakes loose attachment
and carries you further

faster
upon the lush winds of change

Turn your attention always
and above all
to loving your experiences
utterly without judgement
every single breath
and every waking dream

From this state of surrender
you will know
if it is a time to soften into shadow
or rise up into light
for each direction will take you to the other
and back again
until you one day stand tall as the noonday sun
and no earthly thing
will cast darkness
upon your way

AUGUST 2021

On the art of letting go.

Many transmissions reference death, for it is helpful to remind ourselves that we are souls having an embodied journey and thus our mortality is a perception rather than a truth. From this view, death is simply one experience amongst many, a part of one life amongst countless lifetimes.

Physical death is only one form of such a passage. We are familiar with the idea of ego death, the collapse of old protections that no longer serve. But if we look closely, we come to recognize that each lifetime holds within it an ongoing series of deaths and rebirths.

When I observe youthful aspects of myself in this life, I see parts of me that have died, never to return. That which was once unconscious becomes conscious, and consciousness may never be undone. Hidden or buried for a time, perhaps, but never lost.

Once I had a lucid dream wherein I was falling from a great height, just like Nicholas Cage in *City of Angels*. As I plummeted earthward, I could feel the harsh air on my face, pulling my hair straight up with the force of my speed. At first, I panicked and a pure, full-body terror took over. I thought, "This is it. Prepare yourself for the impact, because you are going to die." I waited for the pain, for the immense trauma of hitting the ground, wherever it lay, from whatever great height I had fallen.

It didn't come. I waited; and, still, it didn't come. I continued to fall, more and more, further and further, until I realized there was nothing to hit, no bottom, no end. Then, in that realization, my entire being filled with an ecstatic freedom, beyond gravity, beyond primal fear. I was not flying, but neither was I dying. I was in freefall, in absolute surrender, and blessedly, miraculously, there was no end. This was not a dream about the cruelty of death, but rather a message about the eternal nature of being. If only I would allow.

As you read this transmission aloud, pay attention to any resistance or fear that may arise in your heart or your body. The very possibility of death can be the greatest of teachers, precisely because of the surrender, the softening of the heart and soul that may come when we release our fear of it. There is no freedom like it.

Quick Death

For a glass to break
it must first fall
from a height
and in the shattering
be returned to the dust
from which
it was made

This destruction
must happen
for the form
to be recreated
explosive
yet necessary
for those
who would be
reborn

Do not attempt
to catch the shards

as they fly
but let them burst open
down to the cellular structure
that has been
their definition
and there you will find it
the freedom
the nothingness
you so desire

Do not chase it
but rather take it
as your own
Do not resist it
but rather predispose yourself
to it
Do not pretend
its absence
but rather be unashamed
of it
and as the shattering
continues
you will lose
your awareness of it
as pain
and find instead
that hot peace
burning
in its stead
as you ride the waves
of a fearless pain
relentless
and forgiven
because it is simply

Quick Death

a decomposition
of the old
and is there any greater beauty
than the rotting leaf
that feeds
the buds
of spring

Discover the wisdom
in this beauty
for there lies
your courage
It is everything
as you die
and are born
and you die
and are born
and there is nothing
but exquisite Love
in every crumbling cliff
in every decaying bone
It is your bold celebration
of this truthfulness
that will awaken all
who watch

No more waiting
It is all found
here
where there is no escape
in your surrender
to your sadness
to the reconstruction
of all

that is
your home

Let go
of any life raft
for it is a quick death
that you want
once you welcome
the depths
of the sea

NOVEMBER 2021

Who are you?

This transmission was originally received in the third person, but here I offer it in a first person/mantra format as an active healing tool. As with all received writings, there is such grace given when we speak the words aloud; but this one offers a special opportunity in the use of the two most powerful words in the English language: I AM. When we use these words and utter them aloud, we initiate a powerful energetic opportunity. We reclaim our essential nature and dare to speak it to the world.

Very often I AM statements are used as affirmations, declaring wishes, dreams, and desires, invoking the power of naming that which we hunger to attract. In this transmission, the I AM is used as a tool of detachment, inviting us to release that which does not belong to us, and does not serve.

In my many years as an energy worker and shadow work practitioner, I have learned that the process of release is as fundamental to our expansion as any intent or methods of manifestation. In fact, when we dare to release buried remnants of our wounding, protections and fears, our consciousness is set free to actualize in an organic way, without struggle or manipulation. I think of this as unclogging the log in our human log jam, as release liberates our alignment with the natural karmic flow of all life.

Explore this transmission and observe which stanzas generate a tug at your heart, or stir fear in your belly. These are clues about where attachment may still rule the unconscious and inform behaviours that keep us trapped in an old, small self, which is ready to disassemble. See if you feel more free after digesting the invitation of these words. Who are you, at your core, when the flotsam and jetsam of habitual personality are relinquished?

Shadow work is for the strong, for the humble and the brave. I promise you, as George Addair famously wrote, "Everything you've ever wanted is on the other side of fear."

If I Am Not

I am not my body
I simply borrow it
for a time

I am not my emotions
but they can teach me
then flow through me
and away
like rain upon the roots
of a tree

I am not my mind
and its habits
I am its master
I allow it to serve me well

I am not my fear
although it may try
to convince me otherwise
pretending to keep me safe

long after the danger
has passed

I am not my gifts
they are simply the expression
of Creation
and because they have been given
to me
I am asked to receive them
and value them
with honour

I am not my family
They are fellow soul-travellers
bound to me by a deep
soul love
but I am called
to know my own road

I am not my wounds
nor my suffering
yet my strength and purpose
are forged by these very blows
the diamonds
of my being
born out of
their terrible weight

I am not my longing for a beloved
nor the hunger for the objects of my desires
but rather I am the force
of Love
which these inspire

I am not my morality

If I Am Not

my rules and tenets
agreements and obedience
I am instead
the wild freedom within
an autonomous permission
which can be owned
or stolen
by no man

I am not my ambition
my work
my certificates and degrees
I am not my caste
my skin colour
nor am I my wealth
or poverty
All these are the games and toys
of human days
which utterly dissolve

I am not my stories
my habitual memories
of love lost
of oppression and denial
of powerlessness
and separation from truth
only these are the language
of my realization
They are mine
to rewrite

I am not even my life
for the experience of breath in the body
is the manifestation

of only one brief moment
within my infinite nature
my Presence which may never
be undone

I am also not simply
my fervent meditations and prayers
for Spirit is found
in every moment
conscious or unconscious
of my being
I may ask
If I am not this
then what?
If I am not these aspects
by which I have defined myself
then who?
What remains
when the doings
the personalities
the beliefs all fall away?

If I dare to take this question
deep into my soul
I will find absolute emptiness
waiting for me there
wherein nothingness
the absence of attachment
has made a great space
for Oneness to fill

A place where all separation ends
where lightness and grace
are home

If I Am Not

as they always have been
as they always will be
for the snake of Divine hunger
has swallowed her own tail
until there is nothing but
Creation
free at last

I will return to this place
I must
because in truth
I have never left it
until it came time to remember
who I really am

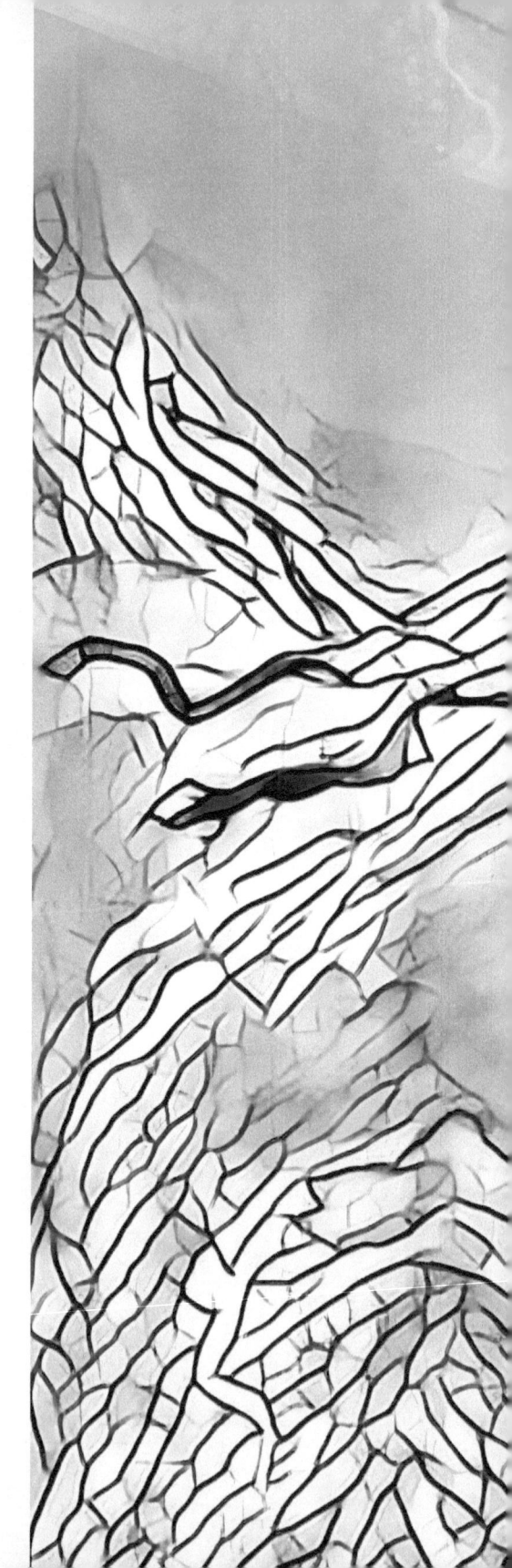

open

JANUARY 2000

The very first transmission.

I had no idea on that winter's night, in the dawning of a new century, the scribblings I found in my journal would lead to such an unfolding, such a relentless calling of my soul purpose.

The more time one spends with a range of transmissions, the more one comes to see that this very first communication holds everything within. While the language of the earlier transmissions tends to be more cryptic, can you see how each image, each reference speaks to the larger principles that are taught in the larger body of work?

Decades of my life and thousands of transmissions later, I still return to these words to ground myself, to root my awareness in the fundamentals of what I now understand to be true.

Please do read this one aloud and feel the richness of the words. The guides tell us that creativity is the new spirituality, and every time we sing, draw, dance, or speak poetry, we are inviting an expression of the soul.

I am grateful that you have followed me through this first compilation of Love Letters, these transmissions of frequency, principles and divine care. I invite you to continue the journey with Book Two in the series, speaking to us of the role of the shadow in our lives and in the world.

Remember: these are not simply writings; they are vibrational tools. Dare to say them in full voice, return to them often, use them in your daily life as reminders that you are never alone. You may find your understanding of the gifts within the words deepens with time, but whomever you are, wherever you are, whenever you read and speak them, these are messages sent to you. They were always meant for you, from the first line written by my pen in the dark. You are loved. You are seen. You are Home.

The Gathering

Under the soil
the earth is calling
calling to the seeds
who sleep
asters, poppies
each will grow in time
can you not feel them?
Each will one day be queen
and the beauty is
they know it not
and no one is Lord
over the other

Children play
do not waken
for dreams are truth
divine
The ancient lives
in the broken seed

DEAR HUMAN CHILD

In your childhood
know that
you are no better than
the seed
fallen in liberty
as the wild goose calls
hoarse with joy

We were taught
to question
yet
ask your mother only one thing

How do I love myself
when I know my
words alone have failed?
Like a
frozen flower
waits
until we know that
for each in turn
once born perfect
once perfect
once grown
perfect to all the
world
And blind faith is the key
blind
and I will hold
only blind
I can still gather you in my arms
and the knowing is in each stick
each leaf
brown and shrivelled
so beautiful

The Gathering

You are forever my children
as the seed
as the seed forever
bursts in my arms

The Gathering

You forgive me?
asks God with a smile
There are whole civilizations
who cannot
and to them
I say
be as this child
her arms full of sticks
whispering
madness

Lie under
the snow blanket
and wait
the promise is made
your turn will come

Out of the dark
and frozen ground
Believe only in
the seed

APRIL 2020

Dare to ask. Dare to claim.
Dare to love.

A s a special gift to you, dear reader, I offer this received prayer. Speak it, sing it, learn it by heart. Feel how each aspect of our human experience is addressed through these simple words. Prayer requires no religion, no technique, no expertise. Prayer is simply a willingness to desire communication with Creator, and to receive support for the expansion of our being.

I say this prayer daily to release stress, to connect with Spirit, and to remind me about what is important in every moment.

I am truly grateful for this life, for every day I live, for every breath I take.

Prayer

I ask that fear be taken from me
that I trust my place in the world
I pray that beauty surrounds me
and my arms be ever open to Love

I claim the Creator within me
I know my joy is a choice
I surrender to the heart which leads me
I allow the sound of my voice
I allow the sound of my voice

I align with the purpose of my calling
I am filled with the freedom to serve
I love myself as I love all of Life
I am grateful for my days upon this Earth
I am grateful for my days upon this Earth

EPILOGUE

THE ANNUAL TRANSMISSION
FOR 2025

A most powerful time to be
alive.

As this volume goes to print, a quarter of a century has passed since Spirit gave new life to the words that flowed from my pen.

What is offered to us here is a fable of the immense gifts of Creation which await, even when we are weary, even in the darkest of hours. The guidance here tells us we are at a tipping point in the soul decisions of the collective, as we achieve a critical mass in consciousness. It seems the moment has arrived.

Will you join us? This invitation is all yours.

The Invitation

Once upon a time
a King and Queen held a great party
He chose the most exquisite foods
to serve
She dressed the hall
with the richest silks upon the walls
and the finest linens upon the tables

Musicians came
who played the music of the gods
The wine was of the most rare
and holy grapes
The royal bees gave of their hives
sacred wax into candles
which lit up the hall
with the light of a thousand stars
and the scent of the honey
of the Goddess
warm and sweet

The Invitation

All was ready
even the masses of fresh flowers
overflowing bowls and vases
in every shade
in colours never before seen
by human eyes

Everything was ready
everything was perfect
and plentiful
and generous
and fine

But no one came

The King waited
his heart open wide
The Queen offered
her arms open wide

But no one came

And so time stopped
the candles paused their burning
the scent of the flowers hung
frozen in time upon the air
and the Eternal said
I will never end
even if I were to wait for you
forever and a day
know this
know this
my candles will always burn

For the people had all been invited
every last soul

had been called to the banquet
for here lay
their very favourite nourishment
for each
and every one

But outside the palace walls
the people were busy
with pursuits of their own
Beyond the gates
of so much plenty
the people were fighting
they were busy with their fighting
because they had so much
to do

The people had fears
they had suffering that they remembered
oh so very well
Their suffering filled their days
and so they fought
they killed to end the killing
they hurt to end the pain
In their hunger
they starved the children of others
and they starved their own children
within

The people left their homes
to seek what they thought
they did not have
and in their seeking
even their homes were lost
The people were so busy

The Invitation

with all that they feared
was missing
and wrong
so busy with what they thought
was gone
the people did not see their invitations
to the most abundant
most loving
most sacred party
that was waiting
just for them

They were too busy
in their fight
over everything they thought
they did not have

But the day came
when a new sun rose
and on the mists
of that dawning morning
an old woman spoke
and she said
Tell them
tell them to listen
but not with their ears
tell them to know
but not with their minds
that there is a royal celebration
and the people are invited
every last one
every man
woman and child

And the words of the elder
rose up over the battlefields
over the factories
over the tall towers
of business and machine
until the words of the invitation
began to float like truth
from a benevolent sky
and somewhere a child replied
There is a party
I am invited
and so
are all of you

The mother listened to her child
and spoke the words with him
I am invited
and so are you
and from the hearth
of their simple home
a light rose
to show them the way
and then a farmer
in the field
heard the invitation
and then a weaver
and a woodworker
and then even a priest of fear
heard the words
as they crumbled his lies
and the light from the hearth rose up
a beacon
a flood light
as the doors of the great hall

The Invitation

were opened even wider
opened wider and brighter
than ever before

For the great King
at one with his powerful Queen
promised they would wait forever
never closing their door
for the party was ready
and the people had heard the invitation
and the music was playing
and the wine was poured
and the feast was waiting
and all that was ever needed
was the willingness to hear
the invitation
and to say

I allow
I accept
I will join in the bounty
I will enter the doors
of infinite celebration

I will come
I am present
I receive
I thank you
I am forgiven
I am worthy
I am loved
I am united and whole

DEAR HUMAN CHILD

The Creator's work
is already done

The party
has begun

Acknowledgments

When a book represents the first collection taken from thousands of transmissions received over a span of twenty-five years, how do I begin to say thank you to all those who have shaped this birth?

I thank my grandmother, Lily, whose Underwood typewriter still sits upon my desk. I thank Ildiko, a friend like no other in my life.

I thank the ones who said these works must be published, and I thank those who did not understand. I thank the readers who cheered, the family I embarrassed, and the dogs who never left my side. I thank the backers who said yes, and the peers who said don't stop. I thank the cupboards full of scribbled journals, the stacks of chaotic papers, the pens that sometimes dried up, but more often made the ink flow. I will never forget the faces of the dear ones who read these transmissions aloud and wept.

I thank my beta readers, video readers, designers, editors, and proof-readers, the visionary ones who reminded me I was not yet fully mad. I thank my beloved children, whom I hope will forgive me for not being some things so I could be another thing, a conduit for Spirit. I thank my many soul sisters for their selfless love, and my community, who rose up to say they wanted to hold this book in their hands. I thank Dan of

Porchlight Book Company, my U.S. distributor, and my literary angel, Amanda, of Awaken Village Press, for making sure I did not walk this path alone.

I thank my spiritual teachers, the pure beings who first opened my heart to a great remembering, and the wise ones, fellow authors, who have paved the way by also daring to listen to their angels and Gods.

But really, I sit in unspeakable gratitude to the guides who have whispered in my ear, over and over and over again, even when it was hard for me to trust. Always present, passionate, and ready to lift me up beyond the cruelties of this world, they are everything, and everywhere. They have never turned me away or said no to me. Not once.

I thank you, my Creator, for coming to me in dreams, visions, and waking moments, ultimately allowing the simple words of this book to make sense of life beyond our clumsy human ways. I am humbled, joyful, and in Love.

Adi Kanda is a Toronto-based author, intuitive, practitioner, and mother of three. Founder of World Without Fear and the Kore Process, she holds decades of experience in deep energy work, releasing karmic patterns at a cellular level. A novelist, actor, poet, and playwright, her received writings from a sleep state have merged into conscious transmissions for thousands of clients and readers worldwide. To learn more, visit: www.worldwithoutfear.org.

Dear Human Child is not just a book but an experience. Discover the activating frequency of the *Dear Human Child* Audio Series as Adi Kanda reads each transmission aloud and purchase the beautiful companion card deck to use powerful transmission excerpts as your personal, daily guide. Simply scan this QR code to access www.dearhumanchild.com.